50p.

SARAH BEENY'S
PRICE
THE JOB

D0995786

COLLINS & BROWN

CONTENTS

INTRODUCTION

HELP!!!

THE JOBS

INTRODUCTION

HOWEVER exciting it may be, building work can be a daunting prospect. Most people are totally at sea when it comes to working out how much a job is going to cost and how long it is going to take. Unless you are very familiar with the building business, estimating the cost of the different jobs involved can be pretty hit and miss. It is essential to be realistic about what is involved and to acknowledge the skills of the various tradesmen you will need to employ. Because most builders are VAT registered you will have to pay an additional 17.5%. If you are a domestic customer, you are unable to reclaim VAT so will have no choice but to pay VAT on all labour and materials.

In an ideal world the best job would be the quickest and the cheapest one too, but unfortunately life isn't like that. The temptation to go for the cheapest quote is often a mistake. If it's done quickly, it may well not be done well. But, just occasionally, speed and quality go hand in hand — so how do you make this happen? The important thing is to find the right person at a good price for the right job. But how?

This book aims to help you by demystifying the building trade. Knowing which contractor does which job can be baffling when you're confronted by the Yellow Pages, which is stuffed with choice. The key thing is to be armed with the right information before you make the first call. That is where I hope this book comes in.

Before You Begin will look at the different trades, and at exactly what they do and how much they charge. If you are living in a city, expect to pay towards the upper end of the price range because there is more demand for good tradesmen, the living expenses and overheads are higher, and there is considerable travel time — sometimes as much as a day in itself — and costs. If you live in a rural area you may not need to spend so much for because the situation is the over way round. Finally, find out how to deal with those crisis moments when you see water dripping through the ceiling, when your heating and hot water suddenly stop working, when a ball smashes through a window or when you've been burgled. What do you check? Who do you call? And what should you expect to be charged to fix it?

The Jobs section simplifies a number of jobs that you may want to do on your house (I have taken a 3-bedroom terraced house and a 4.2 x 4.2m room (14ft x 14ft) as convenient points of reference) and explains what areas are covered by which trades, how long each part of the job is likely to take and how much it's likely to cost. Tradesmen vary in price depending on a large number of factors, from demand to location and their experience. As with any profession, it is very difficult to qualify precisely what makes a good contractor. But in my opinion it's a combination of attention to detail, reliability and degree of much of each of these your contractor has. There is no such thing as the right amount to pay. You will have to judge whether the tradesmen are worth what they are quoting – I am only able to provide guidleines for you to follow.

I hope that **PRICE THE JOB** will help you to clear the fog surrounding general building work that you might want to do on your home, enabling you to be in control the work. One of the most important things, when planning building work, is to make sure you have enough money for the whole job. Don't get carried away buying expensive fixtures and fittings unless you are sure you can afford them. Use this book to work out roughly what you should be paying for a job, but always get written quotes. It is wise to ensure you can fund an extra 10–20% of the costs incase unforeseen problems arise.

Since 1985, the UK has been increasingly using metric units of measurement although imperial units are still occasionally used. Accordingly, I have used metric throughout the book, using imperial only when I felt it was necessary. Be especially careful when working in older houses as existing items (e.g. bricks or pipes) may not match new metrically measured items.

SO GOOD LUCK!

SARAH BEENY April 2006

£

BEFORE
YOU
BEGIN

⌂ WHAT IS A BUILDER?

'Builder' is a convenient catch-all term that covers everything from a main contractor at one end of the scale, to an odd job man right at the other.

MAIN CONTRACTOR Hiring a big main contractor to carry out all the work on your property has the advantage of providing an in-built project manager. He will take the responsibility for everything to do with the job, however big or small. He will organise materials, the sub-contractors, building inspectors' visits, and liaise with your architect, if you employ one. Slang site language sometimes refers to architect's drawings as 'comics' if they have a lack of clarity – not that the architect would be very impressed with this! Generally, a main contractor has more than one job on the go at a time so has a demanding juggling job to make sure men in the company's employ are constantly used and sites run smoothly. The company is responsible for the quality of the work of its sub-contractors, so if anything goes wrong it should deal with it. To cover overheads, it is likely to put a mark-up of at least 15% on the cost of the work.

SUB-CONTRACTOR If you are determined to shoulder the project management yourself, a potentially time-consuming and hair-tearing-out job – especially if you are inexperienced – you will be using specialist sub-contractors or individual tradesmen. Specialist companies cover a specific trade and employ several people skilled in this trade. Again they will put a mark-up of at least 15% on the basic price of the work. Bear in mind that even if the sub-contractors have associations with regulatory bodies, such as CORGI (Confederation for the Registration of Gas Installers), NICEIC (National Inspection Council for Electrical Installation Contracting) or related trade associations, this does not necessarily guarantee the quality of their work. It is still advisable to go by personal recommendation or to follow up references given by previous clients.

SMALL CONTRACTORS There are also smaller contractors who will be able to supply different tradesmen but will not take on the full responsibility of a main contractor. They may well leave dealing with building regulations, the architect's drawings, ordering materials and suchlike to you. Very often builders like this will have a specialist trade of their own, such as plumbing or electrical work, but they will bring in other tradesmen as required.

THE ODD JOB MAN can be the cheapest option as his overheads should be lower than those of any company or contractor. On smaller jobs, he will be able to do the work of a lot of the tradesmen. For example, if it's just a simple job like patching in a bit of blown plaster, he has the advantage of also being able to fit new skirting and decorate the wall. Between you, you will have to make the decision between paying a day rate or a fixed price for the amount of work to be done. You will almost certainly be responsible for getting the right materials to the site on time and you will need to know what the job entails so that you can make decisions when something unforeseen comes up. Odd job men tend to be easier to find in country areas than in cities and are generally less qualified and so cheaper than a specialist.

RATES

SPECIALIST BUILDER: £180–£200 per day

GENERAL BUILDER: £120–£180 per day

LABOURER: £40–£100 per day

ODD JOB MAN: £65–£120 per day

NOTE These prices depend on the level of skill and experience, and locality.

The **odd job man**
is the cheapest option!

CONTACTS Make a note of the builders you approach and the estimates they give you for the work. Don't automatically go for the cheapest and always check the quality of their past work with previous clients.

CONTACTS

Name	Details	£

GROUNDWORKERS

Usually first on the site, the groundworkers are the men who specialise in the work that is done to establish the part of the building that lies below the damp-proof course on the ground floor.

If you are adding an extension to your house, running new drainage or undertaking below groundworks like underpinning, that's where the groundworkers will come in. They will take on any excavation work, putting in the foundations of the building and digging trenches for all the underground utilities i.e. the pipework for running all drains and services. A detailed description of the work and drawings will tell the groundworkers exactly where to excavate for the foundations and pipe runs. Most groundwork deals with drainage or the structure of the building and therefore needs to comply with building regulations. Groundworkers will be familiar with and comfortable working in accordance with these.

RATES

GROUNDWORKER: £200 per day, plus machinery costs. This is an average rate for throughout the country. A labourer will be cheaper.

CONTACTS Keep a record of good tradesmen and their rates –
you never know when it will come in handy for an emergency or to
pass on to others!

Groundworkers work on the part of the building below the damp-proof course!

CONTACTS

Name	Details	£

 BRICKLAYERS OR 'BRICKIES'

Plenty of unqualified bricklayers can lay bricks against a line — a piece of string running from one end of a wall to another — and get the joints equal and the brickwork vertical. However, a more skilled bricklayer can make complicated and detailed joints, and create different decorative effects.

BRICKLAYERS build and repair the internal and external walls of a house, including the chimneys, initially setting out the first courses (a course is a layer of bricks) and damp-proof course, and then building up the courses from there to the roof level. They will also carry out other work such as the construction of garden walls, archways, floors, fireplaces and paving.

RATES

BRICKLAYER: £8 –£250 per day, depending on how many bricks laid per hour and how complex the job.
BRICKLAYER'S LABOURER: £40–£60 per day

Practice makes perfect in the building business. Many bricklayers will lay between 450-600 bricks in an eight-hour day (with a labourer). However, a very experienced bricklayer can lay over 1,200 bricks a day – a massive difference.

SPECIALIST BRICKLAYERS may specialise in stonemasonry cutting and building with stone, but this is an extra skill and will cost you extra money.

CONTACTS

Name	Details	£

⊘ CARPENTERS (JOINERS, CABINET-MAKERS OR CHIPPIES)

Traditionally, there are three different skill areas that fall under this category, with varying specialities and talents.

CARPENTERS carried out the heavy work in the construction of a house, also known as the 'first fix' i.e. cutting and installing the beams, joists, rafters, floorboards and so on.

JOINERS would then come in to complete the 'second fix' – the lighter more detailed work of constructing and fitting the doors and door frames, the window frames and skirting boards.

RATES

CARPENTER: £100–£150 per day
JOINER: £125–£175 per day
CABINET-MAKER: £150–£300 per day depending on the complexity and veneers, jointing, etc.

CABINET-MAKERS are highly trained and skilled craftsmen who design and produce custom-built pieces of furniture, both traditional and contemporary, ranging from fitted bedrooms to bookcases, cabinets, tables, desks, chairs and kitchen units. They can also make minor repairs to an existing piece, French polish it or, if the worst has happened, completely reconstruct it.

MULTI-SKILLED WORKERS Today, with modern tools, less skill may be required and the works of carpenters and joiners is often interchangeable. They are responsible for the carcassing work in kitchens, bedrooms and bathrooms. They also make, install and repair all the structures in the house that are made of wood, such as the stairs, floors, window and door frames, as well as the structural work of the roof, including putting in the roof timbers.

CONTACTS

Name	Details	£

⌂ ROOFERS

If your house is to be kept warm and dry, it's essential to have a watertight roof. Bear in mind that roofing is a seasonal trade and that larger jobs may have to be delayed if the weather is bad.

ROOFERS For any work to your roof, you will need specialist roofers who can repair and replace all roofing systems. They will inspect any leaks coming from the roof, tracing the cause and carrying out damp, water or weather-proofing as necessary. They will be able to strip a section or the whole of an existing roof to check that the underlying roof structure is sound. If working on a pitched and slated or tiled roof, they will lay a breathable waterproof membrane and battens before fixing slates or tiles. They should advise on whether to reuse or replace the existing roof covering. They should also seal edges with lead flashings. They may work with carpenters (on the repairs to the general timber structure of the roof) or with plumbers (on any water or drainage problems).

RATES

ROOFER: £120–£200
The faster and more skilled the roofer, the higher the daily charge is likely to be.

THATCHER: £10,000–£12,000 This depends on the size of the house, materials and complexity of the job.

THATCHERS Straw, water – reed or wheat – reed thatch has been used on roofs for centuries. Today such roofs have a lifespan of between 25-50 years depending on the material, the slope of the roof and the quality of the thatching. The age-old craft of thatching has changed little since medieval times. The thatcher will prepare the material, strip the old roof and check the timbers to see if they need repairing or replacing before attaching the bundles of straw to the roof battens with tarred cord or metal hooks. Do bear in mind that thatched roofs carry a higher fire risk than other roofs and therefore building insurance will not only be more expensive but will need to be obtained through a specialist insurance company. Remember that listed buildings need listed building consent. Generally, all work on roofs will involve scaffolding.

CONTACTS

Name	Details	£

PLUMBERS OR 'FITTERS'

The Latin word for lead is 'plumbum'. Lead was used for plumbing until the 1930s when it was replaced by copper and now sometimes by plastic (although plastic has the disadvantage that it can be eaten by mice!).

PLUMBERS At one time plumbers did all the lead work on site, including cutting the lead to be fitted on a roof. This job is rarely done by them today. Instead they are simply involved in the installation, maintenance and repair of hot and cold water systems both inside and outside the house. This covers plumbing fixtures such as sinks, baths, showers and loos; appliances such as water heaters or boilers; central heating; and complex systems such as sewerage, surface water drainage systems, gas or water pipes. To deal with gas appliances such as hobs, ovens, boilers and water heaters,

RATES

PLUMBER: £100–£250 per day (without CORGI £200), depending on how long the job takes.

plumbers must be registered with CORGI (Confederation for the Registration of Gas Installers). Kitchen sinks, dishwashers and washing machines may be installed by a specialist kitchen supplier. Metal kitchen sinks and baths should be earthed.

CENTRAL HEATING ENGINEERS or boiler repairmen also come under the general heading of 'plumbers' but usually only work within their specialist area. However, an experienced good general plumber should be able to work with both central heating and boilers. Unlike plumbers though, boiler repairmen should have the advantage of carrying loads of spare parts in their van and will use a trial and error method for fixing a problem.

CONTACTS

Name	Details	£

⚙️ ELECTRICIANS OR 'SPARKS'

Thomas Edison invented the first electric light bulb in 1879, bringing lighting into our homes. Today we flick light switches, turn on ovens, run computers and adjust air conditioning and central heating without a second thought.

ELECTRICIANS Making all this possible are the electricians whose job it is to inspect, test and install the domestic electrical wiring system. They are among the first people to come in once a house has been stripped out, in order to put in concealed wiring. The wires are run through the house, connected to circuit-breakers and tested for safety. All the work should be carried out under national and local safety guidelines. New rules introduced in April 2005 specify that you must employ an electrician qualified by the NICEIC (National Inspection Council for Electrical Installation Contracting). Electrical

RATES

ELECTRICIAN: from £100–£250 per day, the longer the job the lower the daily rate.

All **electrical work**
should be carried out
under national and local
safety guidelines!

installations begin to deteriorate after years of extensive use, so if
you are restoring a house, an electrician should check for faulty or
inadequate wiring.

CONTACTS

Name	Details	£

PLASTERERS OR 'SPREADS'

For centuries, plasterers have been responsible for providing different finishes on internal walls, floors and ceilings, both for insulation and so that they can be decorated.

PLASTERERS Plastering is usually in two coats. Originally, both the render coat and the set coat would be lime-based. Lime has the benefit of allowing a wall to breathe but it also has the disadvantage of being very slow to dry, so it can easily be damaged. These days, finding plasterers who will work with lime borders on the impossible. However if you do have an old wall that's prone to damp, it's as well to persevere because the best solution is to use a sand, cement and lime render with a lime skim on the top. If you do use lime plaster on your walls, remember you must use the appropriate paints on

RATES

PLASTERER: £100–£175 per day
LABOURER: £40–£80 per day. You may pay more for specialist or heritage work.

top of it, which will allow the plaster beneath to breathe. Today's fast-moving society demands quick results, so we have become much happier with a 'render and set' that uses gypsum. A plasterer will rarely work alone, so you should cost in a labourer as well.

DRY-LINERS The alternative method of finishing a wall is known as dry-lining. This uses plasterboard – two layers of paper bonded to a central layer of gypsum. The plasterboard is either stuck to the wall using the 'dot and dab' method or screwed to timbers. Then it is taped and filled or set, ready for decoration.

CONTACTS

Name	Details	£

⊖ GLAZIERS

Glass has been around since 3000 BC but glass window panes came into being during the days of Imperial Rome, where they were needed for security and insulation. Little attention was paid to how clear they were. It wasn't until the early 1800s that the first inexpensive rolled window glass became available for large areas. Today glass plays an increasingly important part in twenty-first-century design.

GLAZIERS are responsible for cutting and installing glass panes – although you can easily install single small panes yourself. Nowadays glass is often used in a more sophisticated structural application with metalwork. Painters sometimes double as glaziers because they need to paint the putty afterwards (typical domestic windows are made of timber and the glass is held in place with putty) as well as the window frame. New putty will need to be left to harden for at least a day before it can be painted.

RATES

GLAZIER: £100–£175 per day. Very small jobs may be charged on a one-off fee basis.

GLASS TYPES Most of our older housing stock has 3mm (⅛in) glass for small windows and 4mm, 6mm or even 8mm for larger ones. Glaziers work with a variety of different glass: laminated safety glass (a layer of plastic sandwiched between two panes); toughened safety glass (heat-treated so that it shatters into small pieces when broken); or even glass containing filters to shield against UV rays or heat. The larger glazing firms can also construct double-glazed units.

Be **careful** when handling **cut glass!**

CONTACTS

Name	Details	£

 TILERS

Tiling is an old art form that goes back to pre-Roman times and uses materials varying from ceramic tiles to brick/glass slips, from mosaics to marble. Traditionally a carpenter or painter may well have done this job for you, but tiling has become a specialist trade.

TILER Whether or not you get a tiler in depends on the size of the job. It's probably not worth it just for a splashback but if you are doing a whole floor, wall or other significant area, an experienced tiler will do the job much faster than a non-specialist. Not only that, the finish will almost certainly be much, much better. Yes, he will cost more than your builder but will be in and out of the site like a flash, having brought the right tools and skill. It can make the difference between one day or two weeks on the job.

RATES

TILER: £80–£200 per day
ODD JOB MAN: £65–£120 per day. Use a tiler for more complicated or extensive work. The higher the rate, the quicker and more skilled the tiler should be.

Tilers generally work in teams but without other tradesmen. A trained tiler will know exactly how to achieve the best finish, preparing the surface properly before he begins and using the right adhesive and grout.

An **experienced tiler** will do the job much **faster** than a non-specialist!

There are various adhesives and mortars to fix tiles to a surface, and different types of grout for different applications. Take advice from your supplier, or ask your tiler, if you are not sure which type you need for a particular job.

CONTACTS

Name	Details	£

⊖ PAINTERS AND DECORATORS

This must be one of the most undervalued trades, simply because everyone thinks they can do it themselves. In fact the paint finish – the bit that is seen – is the one thing that makes the difference between a good job and a bad job. A really good decorator can transform an unattractive house while a bad decorator can ruin a lovely one. This is the one area where people think they can cut costs – often with disastrous results.

PAINTER Most people are under the impression that they are paying a painter to paint. They may feel rather cheated when their painter spends four days making a mess as they sand bits down and make good any holes or rough bits before spending only one day painting. In fact, 80% of the time spent on a decorating job should be spent on preparation. It is worth every minute if you want a good finish.

RATES

PAINTER: £80–£150
SPECIAL PAINT EFFECTS:
£250–£450, depending on level of skill required.

SPECIALIST DECORATORS Since fashion has led the move away from wallpaper to paint finishes, plenty of inexperienced and untrained painters and decorators have set up in business. Hanging paper requires skill whereas anyone can throw some emulsion around a house – although not always as successfully as you might like. Traditionally, all decorators would be skilled in all paint effects. This is less common now.

Always check your decorator's credentials with previous employers.

CONTACTS

Name	Details	£

CARPET-LAYERS AND FITTERS

One of the most satisfying finishing touches to give a room is to have the floor covering laid. Unless you are opting for tiles or wood, you will probably need the services of a good carpet-layer.

CARPET-LAYER The carpet layer will take up and remove any existing carpet. (You can save yourself some money by doing this yourself.) Then he will prepare the surface, possibly levelling it or sealing it, before cutting and laying underlay or hardboard. Finally he will lay the carpet, cutting and fitting it, stitching or taping joins where necessary, stretching it over spiked grippers at the wall edges and fixing door strips (available in different finishes) or stair runners. Alternatively, he will prepare the floor before gluing/heat-sealing (whichever is appropriate) the flooring – carpet tiles, lino, cork, rubber sheeting or wood laminate.

RATES

CARPET LAYER: £90–£160 per fitter per day, if not included in carpet price. You may need two men to move heavy furniture, in which case one experienced fitter and a labourer would be cheaper than two fitters.

Once you have chosen the flooring, (carpet or vinyl tiles, lino, cork, rubber sheeting or wood laminate), it's the carpet-layer's job to come and measure up the area and to calculate how much of the chosen floor covering you'll need. Alternatively you can draw an exact floor plan of the room, including all the measurements, to take to the carpet shop so they will be able to work out how much material you need. They will also work out how to cut the material so that it is used as cost-effectively as possible, while making sure that any patterns match up exactly. Once you have approved their estimate, a carpet-layer will arrive to lay the flooring – he will work much faster if you have cleared the room of all loose furniture.

CONTACTS

Name	Details	£

£ FINDING THE RIGHT MAN FOR THE JOB

There are plenty of cowboys in the building trade who are ready to rip you off at the first opportunity. How can you insure yourself against falling victim to them? The surest way is to follow personal recommendation, so start by asking friends and neighbours if they can help. If you run up against a brick wall, try one or two trade associations for a list of members in your area. The Federation of Master Builders runs a great website called www.findabuilder.co.uk.

GOOD EMPLOYER On the other side of the coin, for every cowboy there is a potentially bad employer. To get the best from your builder, make sure you are not one of them. Be prepared to brief him precisely in writing about the job; agree a price for the job and the stages at which you will be paying; pay up accordingly; try not to change your mind halfway through; expect to pay for any modifications to the original plan; and let him get on with the work without distractions from you. Agree whether they will be removing all building rubbish at the end of each day or at the end of the job.

GETTING QUOTES Select three contractors and ask them to give you a written quote for the work. Also ask them for three references and follow them up, asking previous employers whether they were happy with the job they did and, if possible, go to look at the quality of their workmanship yourself. It's wise to do all this even if they come with the highest recommendation. Check their insurance cover by asking to see their builder's liability insurance certificate.

THE AGREEMENT Once you've decided on your contractor, make a written agreement that specifies the work to be done in as much detail as possible, right down to the clearing away of rubbish. The agreement should name the price agreed, including VAT and the payment stages. Be cautious about paying for anything in advance – including a deposit. The contract should set a start and completion date with penalty clauses if the work runs over. It should stipulate any special instructions, including how to deal with those inevitable extras. Both parties must agree how much it will cost and both sign the agreement. Extras should only crop up for two main reasons – if an unforeseen problem arises or simply because you change your mind. It is easy to rack up large sums without realising, so make it very clear that any extra costs should be agreed before additional work is carried out. This way no dispute should ever arise.

WORKING OUT EXACTLY
WHAT YOU WANT DONE

It is worthwhile taking time to think through exactly what work you want done on your house so that you're confident about explaining it to someone else. Answering the following questions will help.

- What are you trying to achieve?
- What look are you trying to achieve?
- Is there any other work in your house that you would like to be done at the same time as the main job?
- Are you going to be buying the materials or do you want your contractor to do it?
- If you are, do you know which materials and the quantities?
- Will you source the materials at this stage (It may well be worth it.) and know when they are needed?
- How long will each job take?
- In what order should the jobs be done?
- Which tradesman will be responsible for each job?
- Make a timetable so that you can see who should arrive when, what they need, and whether you will need to delay them if your schedule slips. Try to give them as much warning as possible if this happens.

NOTES

Trade	Job	Time Estimate	Start Date

MAKE THINGS EASIER FOR YOURSELF

Give yourself time to get quotes and ensure you have the relevant approvals and book the work in fit around whatever you are doing.

➡ Don't rush into having work done if it's going to disrupt your life. Instead of cramming it into the two weeks before you go on holiday, allowing no room for delays, it might be easier on the nerves to go on holiday and start the builder on your return. It will be a more relaxing experience if you can wait until the time and weather is right.

➡ Any building work is likely to cause a certain amount of dust and disruption, therefore empty the rooms where work is to be done. It's worth buying a roll of thick polythene (DPM) to cover carpets, taping it to the skirting, to protect books in bookcases and to seal up doorways if you don't need to use them.

➡ Be firm but fair with your builder. Keep talking to him about every aspect of the job, however small. Bad communications can lead to disputes, which are often very difficult to solve amicably. Generally, both parties end up dissatisfied.

WHAT ARE YOU PAYING FOR?

When you employ a tradesman, bear in mind exactly what you are paying for. It may not cost you very much to change a washer but if you call a plumber to do the job, it will cost much more. Why? This list is what he is charging for – and you should be prepared to pay.

- His skills
- The full range of specialist equipment
- Obtaining the materials for the job
- Transport and parking
- Time on the job
- Clearing up and packing away
- Business overheads

Before he arrives, make sure you know exactly what you want him to do. The main problem may be your leaking loo, but before you call a plumber check that there isn't anything else that you have put off doing that you would like him to fix while he is there. When you call him, itemise everything – however trivial. If you start adding extra things to do after he arrives, do not be surprised when he charges you for them and your bill is much higher than his original estimate.

⊕ RULES AND REGULATIONS

Building work needs to comply with the relevant rules and regulations. All these lie within the remit of the planning department of your local authority. If in doubt, you can make an initial verbal or written enquiry to the planning department, to find out whether the work you plan to do needs to comply with any regulations and, if so, which ones. Even if you don't need planning permission, you will still need to comply with any relevant building regulations. Exceptional cases might involve listed buildings, work in conservation areas, or change of use (from barn to house, for example).

➤ Planning permission deals with the way a building looks and its effect on the local environment. You can apply for planning permission in two stages – outline and then detailed – but you will need detailed drawings to accompany the application, so unless you are very experienced it is best to get an expert to submit an application for you. Submit an application in good time – it may take a while to to be approved.

➡ Building regulations deal with the safety, structure and function of a building and with its environmental impact (insulation etc). You can either submit a building notice, if you are doing minor works, or submit a full planned application for more major works. It is best to ask your builder/architect to be responsible for any compliance with building regulations.

➡ Some properties are listed buildings or in a conservation area and you will need special permission to do work. Both these will fall under the remit of the conservation department in your local planning office.

WARNING! It is a criminal offence to carry out works without the relevant permissions.

TOP FIVE STEPS
TO GETTING
A JOB DONE...

1 **Work out** what you want done.

2 **Break down** the jobs to see what each part entails.

3 **Prepare** drawings and lists of works.

4 **Source** the right contractor.

5 **Source** the materials.

FIVE KEY THINGS

TO AVOID...

1 **Starting your job too early** with lack of preparation.

2 **Not giving the contractor** enough space to work in.

3 **Talking on the clock –** if you talk too much to the builder, you will pay for it.

4 **Changing your mind** and asking for 'while-you're-heres'.

5 **Over or under-paying.**

TOP FIVE THINGS

A CONTRACTOR

SHOULD AVOID...

1 **Overbooking himself**
and not turning up on time.

2 **Underestimating**
the length of time a job is
going to take.

3 **Bad communication.**

4 **Leaving the job
unfinished.**

5 **Expecting** to be paid for
work they haven't done.

⌂ EMERGENCY REPAIRS

You will be charged a premium for an emergency call-out. Is the problem really as bad as you think? Look at what has happened calmly and clearly, checking whether you can deal with it yourself or at least limit the damage before calling out an expert.

LEAKING PIPE

- ➡ Turn off the water at mains stopcock.
- ➡ Then run the taps to drain the system.
- ➡ Turn off the electricity if the leak runs close to wiring or electrical fittings.
- ➡ If punctured by a nail, leave the nail in place.
- ➡ Call a plumber.

EMERGENCY CALL-OUT FEE: £20–90 (may include between 15–60 mins labour time) plus cost of work and parts. An hourly rate will be loaded for an emergency.

DON'T PANIC

BLOCKED SINK OR DRAIN

➡ If the waste pipe from a basin or sink is blocked, try a plunger.

➡ Place a bucket under the basin or sink, open the trap in the pipe and poke wire down to clear blockage.

➡ Try a proprietary drain cleaner

➡ Call a plumber/drainage company.

EMERGENCY CALL-OUT FEE: £80–170 (may include between 15–60 mins labour time) plus cost of work and parts.

CISTERN PROBLEMS

➡ Take the top of the cistern off and see whether the ball cock is jammed.

➡ Shut off the water supply to cistern.

➡ Hold flush down until cistern is empty.

➡ If flushing system needs replacing, take mechanism to plumber's merchant so you can buy the correct one.

➡ If this doesn't work, call the plumber.

EMERGENCY CALL-OUT FEE: £20–90 (may include between 15–60 mins labour time) plus cost of work and parts.

BLOCKED LOO

➡ Use a plunger to try to loosen blockage.

➡ If it clears, flush loo several times to wash through.

➡ Open manhole cover and try rodding the blockage loose.

➡ If you can't clear it, you will need to call a drainage company who will have various sophisticated tools for removing the blockage.

EMERGENCY CALL-OUT FEE: See Leaking pipe

CRISIS!!!

GAS FAULT

This is a potentially deadly situation. Natural gas doesn't smell but suppliers add a smell as a safety precaution.

➡ If you smell gas, open the doors and windows.

➡ Extinguish any naked flames.

➡ Turn off all gas appliances.

➡ Do not use electrical switches, smoke or light a match.

➡ Telephone British Gas or a CORGI-registered plumber.

EMERGENCY CALL-OUT FEE: £50–110, usually includes 15–60mins labour, after which an hourly charge.

CHANGING LOCKS

→ Taking a locks to a locksmith saves a call-out fee.

→ If there are two locks, change one at a time.

→ Take the first lock to the locksmith's, change it and fit it before taking the second lock.

→ Locks vary in size. Replacement is much quicker and easier if the new one fits the existing hole exactly.

→ Or call locksmith to come to your house.

EMERGENCY CALL-OUT FEE: £30–90 (usually includes 15–60 mins labour) plus parts. An hourly rate will be loaded for an emergency.

BROKEN WINDOWS

→ If a break-in, call the police to check for fingerprints.

→ Carefully remove the broken glass.

→ Tape polythene or card over the hole temporarily.

→ Call a glazier.

EMERGENCY CALL-OUT FEE: No call out fee unless windows need to be boarded, in which case £50–120.

THE
JOBS

FITTING A NEW KITCHEN

Kitchens are the most expensive room in the house to fit out. There are numerous sources for the units: specialist suppliers, joiners, kitchen unit manufacturers, department stores and DIY stores. Look at a good selection of what is available before making a choice.

THERE ARE VARIOUS TYPES OF KITCHEN UNITS AVAILABLE:

▶ **FLAT PACK** This is normally the cheapest option, but if your kitchen comes as a flat pack, remember to cost in the time of making up the carcasses.

▶ **READY MADE** Proprietary brand kitchens are usually delivered mostly assembled, and the company will offer an installation service.

▶ **BESPOKE** This is the top end of the market and units are built especially for you and to fit the room. The company will come and fit the kitchen and you can have exactly what you want.

Most kitchens are fitted but others are freestanding (the furniture is not attached to the walls). Prices vary enormously. To help you decide where to go, first decide on your budget and work out exactly what you need to include in your kitchen. When it comes to designing the layout, the kitchen supplier will do it for you, or you may want to ask your joiner to help. If you have a dishwasher, it is a good idea to plan the storage of the crockery and cutlery around its position.

Kitchen suppliers may offer one unit (e.g. a 1000mm base unit) very cheaply to lure you into buying a particular kitchen. But beware... **Price the whole kitchen** before committing yourself because they may load the price on other items you need from them.

TOP TIPS
FOR DESIGN...

1 **Organise different work areas** to minimise movement between them.

2 **Work out your storage** needs carefully so that things are in easy reach of where you need them most.

3 **Doors and drawers** should open and shut freely.

4 **Save money** by having cheap carcasses but finish the units off with more expensive doors and good handles.

5 **Spend more on the worktops** and less on the units.

6 **Good lighting is vital,** especially over all the work surfaces, including the hob and sink.

⌂ KITCHEN PLAN

Once you have decided on all the appliances you want to include, draw a scale plan of your proposed kitchen to work out the most efficient way to incorporate them into your design.

SAMPLE PLAN

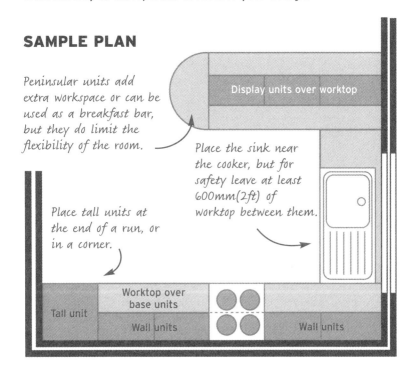

Peninsular units add extra workspace or can be used as a breakfast bar, but they do limit the flexibility of the room.

Display units over worktop

Place the sink near the cooker, but for safety leave at least 600mm(2ft) of worktop between them.

Place tall units at the end of a run, or in a corner.

Tall unit

Worktop over base units

Wall units

Wall units

MY PLAN AND NOTES

⊕ APPLIANCE PLANNER

APPLIANCE	✔	£	££	£££
BUILT-IN OVEN				
Single		£150	£250	£1,000
Double		£380	£500	£1,300
HOB				
4-ring electric		£90	£120	£230
4-ring gas		£90	£130	£230
Ceramic hob		£170	£300	£600
Microwave		£50	£400	£750
Dishwasher		£170	£350	£620
Fridge/freezer		£160	£300	£600
Washing machine		£170	£230	£450
Tumble dryer		£100	£190	£250
Boiler (see Fitting a boiler, page 132)		£1,300	£1,600	£1,900

APPLIANCE	✔	£	££	£££
SINGLE SINK				
Stainless steel		£38	£52	£150
Other		£100	£190	£240
DOUBLE SINK				
Stainless steel		£170	£200	£430
Other		£200	£450	£650
Waste disposal unit		£160	£270	£440
TAPS				
Mixer		£39	£60	£150
Single (price per pair)		£20	£36	£45
Special hose fitting		£135	£200	£300
Filter		£150	£200	£330
EXTRACTOR				
To exterior		£80	£250	£500
Recirculating		£80	£250	£500

UNITS

An average-size kitchen 4.2x4.2m (14x14ft) will need housing for a built-in oven, 4 x 1000mm base units, 4 x 1000mm wall units, kickboards and a worktop – depending on the design and budget.

TYPICAL BASE UNIT

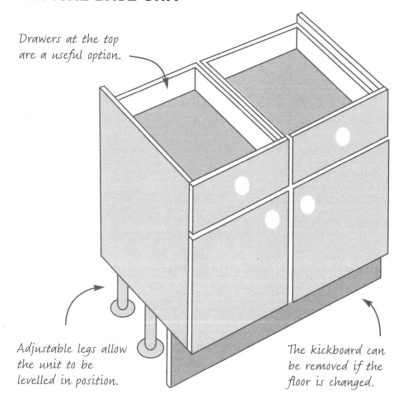

Drawers at the top are a useful option.

Adjustable legs allow the unit to be levelled in position.

The kickboard can be removed if the floor is changed.

UNIT	Number	£	££	£££
BASE UNITS				
300mm		£20	£80	£255
400mm		£25	£85	£280
500mm		£30	£90	£300
600mm		£35	£100	£350
800mm		£40	£145	£420
1000mm		£70	£155	£450
DRAWER UNITS				
400mm		£75	£225	£620
600mm		£100	£325	£675
APPLIANCE UNIT		£100	£570	£620
WALL UNITS				
300mm		£15	£75	£240
400mm		£20	£80	£250
500mm		£25	£85	£255
600mm		£30	£95	£340
800mm		£35	£140	£430

WORKTOP	Length	£	££	£££
Corian, per metre		£300	£380	£400
Granite, per metre		£50	£100	£190
Woodblock, per metre		£23	£60	£100
Laminate, per metre		£10	£30	£55
KICKBOARDS		£5	£20	£29
SPLASHBACK				
Tiles, per square metre		£4	£10	£20
Stainless steel, per square metre		£30	£80	£100
Mosaic tiles, per square metre		£30	£40	£70

REMEMBER YOU NEED SOCKETS FOR

- [ ] Power supply to boiler
- [ ] Power supply to oven
- [ ] Fridge
- [ ] Freezer
- [ ] Tumble dryer
- [ ] Washing machine
- [ ] Dishwasher
- [ ] Toaster
- [ ] Kettle
- [ ] Coffee-maker
- [ ] Blender
- [ ] Microwave
- [ ] TV
- [ ] Stereo
- [ ] Telephone/answering machine
- [ ] 4 miscellaneous

TRADES YOU WILL NEED

CARPENTER

2-5 DAYS to install the units. If the kitchen comes as a flat pack, add an extra day for making the carcasses before they can be installed.

PLUMBER

1-3 PART-days. One to run the pipe work and another to connect it when the kitchen has been fitted. If your kitchen appliances are in totally new places, then the plumber may well need more time for boxing in.

ELECTRICIAN

1-3 DAYS, depending on how many sockets need to be fitted and whether the lighting is to be changed.

TILER

1 DAY for the splashbacks, if required; 1-4 days for tiling the floor.

SEE CARPENTERS p20–21, PLUMBERS p24–25
ELECTRICIANS p26–27, TILERS p32–33 ▶

CHANGING A BATHROOM

There's nothing more satisfying than replacing a tired old bathroom with a sparkling new one. It doesn't have to cost the earth.

PLANNING To keep the costs down, keep the loo in the same place. If you decide to move it, you will have the extra expense of moving the soil pipe to accommodate it. The bath, basin and shower run through a smaller waste pipe which, although it needs a fall, is much easier to run from different positions in the room. Otherwise decide whether you want to add any extra features such a bidet or a shower, and see whether you have to move the siting of anything else to fit.

ACCESSORIES When you're pricing a bathroom, don't forget the accessories that you may need – taps, heated towel rail, shower accessories (see Installing a shower, page 80), mirror, shaving sockets, shaving light, and so on – because they all mount up. There is an enormous choice on the market, vastly ranging in price. This is one area where you need to do your groundwork.

COLOUR It is amazing how many different shades of white there are. You may find that white bathroom fittings do not always exactly match each other and this can look really disappointing in a newly finished bathroom. The best way to avoid a mismatching bathroom is to buy a complete bathroom suite, which often ends up being cheaper than buying the items individually. You can also try to find pieces in a reclamation yard to suit the period of your house. It is best to buy these at the same time to avoid colour problems. Be warned though – taking old taps and old wastes off reclaimed bathroom fittings can be very difficult and there is always a danger that something will break in the process.

LIGHTING AND HEATING are important considerations. One key thing to remember is that all unfused switches and sockets, apart from a shaving socket, should be situated outside a bathroom.

FLOORING AND WALL COVERINGS are another consideration. Tiles are the obvious solution, because they are waterproof and easy to clean. I would steer clear of carpet here, because it can get damp and smelly. Wood flooring is a possibility, but it must be well sealed so that any moisture cannot penetrate. Vinyl is also a practical alternative.

TOP TIPS
FOR BATHROOM
DESIGN...

1 **When positioning the bath**, make sure there's enough room for you to get out and dry yourself comfortably.

2 **Make sure there is enough room** around each end of the bath for you to turn the taps on and off easily without scraping your knuckles, and, lie comfortably in the bath with your head relaxed on the back.

3 **Allow space in front** of and beside both the loo and the bidet so you can sit comfortably (or stand without hitting your head on the eaves!) and so that it is easy to clean around.

4 **Make sure** there is plenty of headroom in front of the basin so that you can wash or use the mirror comfortably; allow space behind you so that you can bend over it easily.

5 **If you are installing a shower**, allow at least a metre in front of it so you have enough room to stand and dry yourself.

SAMPLE BATHROOM PLAN

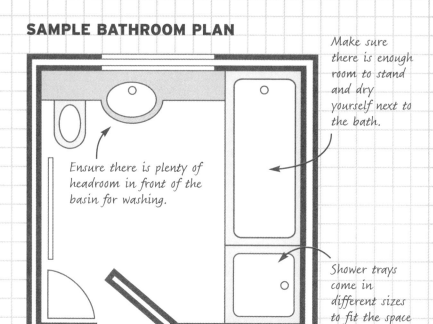

Make sure there is enough room to stand and dry yourself next to the bath.

Ensure there is plenty of headroom in front of the basin for washing.

Shower trays come in different sizes to fit the space available.

MY PLAN AND NOTES

Don't forget about installing the electrics for a light above the mirror, electric toothbrush and shaving socket if required.

ESSENTIALS	£	££	£££
BATH			
Built-in	£110	£150	£190
Freestanding	£250	£400	£800
BASIN			
Pedestal	£80	£150	£250
Wall-mounted	£40	£90	£180
Underslung to a vanity top	£50	£80	£150
PAN			
Wall mounted	£150	£250	£400
Freestanding	£80	£200	£400

ESSENTIALS	£	££	£££
CISTERN			
Standard	£40	£125	£200
Concealed	£60	£90	£150
High level	£60	£100	£200
Loo seat	£10	£35	£90
BIDET			
Wall-mounted	£90	£200	£400
Freestanding	£80	£200	£400
TAPS			
Individual sink (per pair)	£40	£140	£300
Monoblock sink	£60	£185	£400
Individual bath (per pair)	£40	£180	£600
Monoblock bath	£75	£250	£800
HEATED TOWEL RAIL			
Electric	£100	£300	£1,000
Mains	£90	£300	£800

SEE INSTALLING A SHOWER p80-85 ▶

TRADES YOU WILL NEED

PLUMBER

1–3 DAYS, depending on whether the soil pipe is lifted. If moving the location of any of the items within the same room, you need to add 2–3 days of a plumber's time.

CARPENTER

2 DAYS, to box in the bath and any new pipework. Allow an extra day if plywood has to be laid over the floor.

TILER

2 DAYS, the first to lay the tiles and the second to grout them after the adhesive has had a chance to dry.

DECORATOR

2 DAYS, the first for preparation and the second for painting. Allow another day if there is a large amount of making good to be done or if the room is very large.

SEE PLUMBERS p24–25, **CARPENTERS** p20–21; **TILERS** p32–33, **DECORATORS** p34–35 ▶

⊕ INSTALLING A SHOWER

Showers are very fashionable although I personally find it hard to understand why anyone would want one. Some people think that getting wet and cold is a nice thing to do! It seems to me that they always leak, cause condensation and go mouldy, BUT there's no doubt that they make the most efficient use of water for washing.

WATER PRESSURE A decent shower depends on having enough constant hot water. Before you decide to fit one ask your plumber to check the water pressure (if it will run from the mains) to ensure there's enough pressure to make it effective. The solution to a lack of pressure lies in either using water from a well − positioned tank and/or installing a pump. The other important factor is flow rate. If you are relying on mains pressure, your options include installing an electric shower, a combination boiler or a thermal − store cylinder. However, the flow may be too slow to give a really good shower and the temperature may vary when another tap in the house is turned on or someone flushes the loo. Then the only solution is to increase the size of the incoming mains − an expensive job.

▶ SHOWER CUBICLE This can be made to fit the space you have available and can be fitted with any kind of shower. You will need a shower tray, probably in either porcelain or plastic. Trays come in a variety of sizes and shapes to fit most spaces and almost all have an upstand of about 150mm. Fit the tray into an existing alcove, against a wall or into a corner. Shower enclosures to fit around the tray come in a corresponding range of designs. Doors can bi-fold, hinge, pivot or slide. Glass can be clear, frosted, patterned: you name it. A shower curtain is a less reliable, alternative to an enclosure.

▶ WET ROOM The wet room is fully tiled on the floor and walls and water runs away through a floor drain. Again it can accommodate any type of shower, but you can dispense with the shower tray and enclosure. The key elements to its success are a well tiled wall and a slightly sloping floor so the room drains easily.

▶ SHOWER CABIN A self-contained shower cabin is the simplest but most expensive option. However it should guard against any leakages and will come with all sorts of fancy additions such as body jet systems and steam treatments.

SEE BATHROOM p72–79, **PLUMBERS** p24–25 ▶

TYPES OF SHOWER There are several different kinds of shower fitting that you can install.

▶ **PRESSURE-BALANCED MIXER SHOWER** This provides a more stable temperature but it can be subject to fluctuation. It can be used with a combination boiler.

▶ **THERMOSTATIC MIXER SHOWER** This will guarantee against variations in temperature and flow rate. It can be used with a gravity fed shower but may need to be paired with a booster pump. It can also be used with a combination boiler.

▶ **POWER SHOWERS** are most people's preferred option. The name describes a shower with excellent water pressure. To have maximum pressure, you need to have pipework carrying a large-diameter volume of water, plus good pressure for that water. This, combined with a powerful pump, makes for a great shower. For the ultimate results, combine one with a thermostatic mixer.

▶ **TOWER SHOWER** An alternative to a standard wall shower fitting is the all-singing and all-dancing tower shower, which offers hand and fixed showerheads, body showers and shelving units.

INSTALLATION The most important thing is to make sure that a shower is properly sealed, as one of the highest instances of domestic insurance claims is for damage caused by leaking showers. Reassure yourself that your builder is using waterproof plywood or board behind the tiles. The key areas where leaking occurs are at the joint between the wall and shower tray, around the shower fixture or through faulty grouting. One way of preventing problems with tiles is to use single sheets of glass or mirror, which limits potential leaking to just corner and floor/wall joints. A silicone sealer should be put on the joints before the

I would run a line of **silicone** around the shower tray before tiling and then again afterwards – **seal and seal** again.

SHOWER AREAS	£	££	£££
SHOWER CUBICLE			
Shower tray	£100	£175	£300
Shower enclosure	£450	£525	£600
Shower curtain	£30	£60	£300
Shower screen	£90	£300	£1,200
Accessories	£20	£100	£300
WET ROOM			
Tiling, per square metre	£200	£400	£600
Accessories	£20	£100	£300
SHOWER CABIN	£450	£525	£600

SHOWER FITTINGS	£	££	£££
Pressure-balanced mixer shower	£50	£220	£500
Thermostatic mixer shower	£80	£250	£700
Power shower	£140	£280	£450
Tower shower	£140	£300	£1,500
Pump	£150	£200	£350

TRADES YOU WILL NEED

TILER

2 DAYS, the first to prepare and tile the walls, and the second to grout so they are thoroughly water – resistant.

ELECTRICIAN

1 DAY, if required, to install electrics for the shower or pump.

PLUMBER

1 DAY, to install the drainage and the water supply to the shower. If the shower is being installed away from an existing supply, allow extra time.

DECORATOR

2 DAYS, one to prepare and make good, and one to decorate around the outside of the shower. If there is only a very small area to be redecorated, this may be done in one day.

SEE TILERS p32–33, **ELECTRICIANS** p26–27, **PLUMBERS** p24–25, **DECORATORS** p34–35 ▶

◇ TILING A BATHROOM

Decorative tiles have been around for centuries, used on the exterior of buildings as well as the interior. Visit Roman ruins, Turkish mosques or walk through the streets of Lisbon to see plenty of wonderful examples.

TILES make a great finish for a bathroom – on the wall, on the floor and even on the ceiling. They are waterproof, easy to clean, hard-wearing and can bring colour and light into a room. There is an almost limitless range of shapes, sizes, colours and patterns available; sizes range from large ceramic tiles to tiny mosaics in a variety of materials, while more interesting shapes include rectangular tiles, which can be laid either horizontally or vertically, and hexagonal tiles.

The longer a ceramic tile has been baked, the harder and more water resistant it becomes. The hardest are known as 'vitreous' and are impervious to water. Glazing a non-vitreous tile helps it become more water resistant, although water can still penetrate the unglazed sides and back.

TILE SIZE	Quantity per sq m	+ 10% wastage
100x100mm (4x4in)	100	110
150x150mm (6x6in)	49	54
200x200mm (8x8in)	25	28
300x300mm (12x12in)	16	18
100x200mm (4x8in)	50	55

When planning a tiling layout across an entire wall, find the centre-line of the wall and work outwards. If the number of tiles does not fit exactly, having an equal-sized part-tile at each end will look better than having a full tile at one end and an oddment at the other.

QUANTITIES Measure the dimensions of all the areas that you are tiling in order to work out (or to ask the tile supplier to work out) how many tiles you need. Tile a wall up to the ceiling for a more clinical effect. Order about 10% more tiles than necessary to allow for breakages when cutting.

INSTALLATION All tiles must be laid on a clean, dry, flat surface, and stuck with special adhesive or, occasionally, mortar. Once the adhesive has had a chance to dry and the tiles are firmly in place, waterproof grout is applied between the gaps.

GROUT If the grout in a bathroom is cracking up or mouldy, there are various ways you can try to refresh it. You can scrape it out and regrout, but this is time-consuming and it is very difficult to get a good finish. You can bleach the existing grout, though this is not always effective. Or you can buy a white colourant to paint over the grout – but in my experience this gives a short-lived and not particularly effective result. The long and short of it is: if you want a perfect finish for tiling, you need to remove the existing tiles and start from scratch.

FLOOR TILES If you are tiling the bathroom floor, remember that tiles with a smooth glaze can be slippery when wet, so you might prefer to look for a rougher glaze. If you are laying tiles on floorboards, you will need to lay waterproof plywood, 9mm thick, before tiling. You may have to lift the loo and the basin if using thicker tiles, and trim the bottom off the bathroom door. If there is an existing loo, basin and bath in place, I would advise using as thin a tile as possible so that you can avoid lifting the bathroom suite. If you are planning a combination of plain and patterned tiles, or are using tiles to create a pattern, make a paper pattern to scale so the tiler can see exactly what you want. It's a bore to have to remove tiles and start again.

PRICES

Tiles are generally sold by the square metre. To work out the square meterage that you require, take each area that you want covered and multiply the vertical measurement by the horizontal measurement. Then add each area together to get the total square meterage, adding 10% to allow for breakages.

TILES PER SQ M	£	££	£££
Mosaic	£10	£60	£120
Standard 150x150mm (6x6in)	£4	£30	£80
Oversize 200x200mm (8x8in)	£15	£40	£90
Marble slips	£42	£50	£70

If you're using **unsealed** tiles, set them out on the floor and seal them before laying and **grouting**. Seal again afterwards.

TRADES YOU WILL NEED

LABOURER		1 DAY, hacking off the old wall tiles. If there is only a small area this may be done by the tiler.
PLASTERER		1 DAY, for patch plastering and making good after the old tiles have all been removed.
CARPENTER		1 DAY, to lay plywood (if this is required) before the new flooring can be laid.
TILER		2 DAYS, the first to lay the tiles and the second to grout them after the adhesive has had a chance to dry.
PLUMBER		1–3 DAYS – to move the fittings, if necessary, and replace them after the tiles have been finished.

SEE LABOURERS p12–15, **PLASTERERS** p28–29, **CARPENTERS** p20–21, **TILERS** p32–33, **PLUMBERS** p24–25 ▶

⊕ POURING A CONCRETE FLOOR

If you're moving into an old house, the chances are that it may well not have a damp-proof course or insulation in the ground floor/basement. The front rooms of many old houses had suspended floors with vents at the front and back of the building for airflow.

CONCRETE FLOOR If you have to install a completely new floor throughout, you may consider using concrete. This is a very dirty and dusty job so shield the rest of the house as thoroughly as you can. The old floor will have to be removed before using compacted hardcore to create a level surface, with sand rolled flat on top. A damp-proof membrane (a thick polythene sheet) is laid across the floor with the sides turned up at the walls. This will prevent moisture seeping up from the ground. Concrete is then poured (it can be delivered ready-mixed) on top of the membrane to make a slab and finished off with a thin layer (screed) of sand and cement.

REINFORCED CONCRETE Depending on the thickness of the concrete, reinforcing rods may need to be laid in it. Insulation board can be laid below or above the concrete. If above, the screed is laid over the board. The edges of the membrane can be trimmed and hidden behind the skirting board.

REGULATIONS All this work should be done in liaison with the local Building Inspector, who will be able to advise on how much thermal insulation is needed.

FLOOR FINISH Tiles can be laid directly on the concrete or the screed. Instead of laying a concrete floor, you can fit a semi-suspended floor over the concrete slab, although take into account the fact that the ceiling height may be reduced.

PRICE PER SQ M	£	££	£££
Ready-mixed concrete	£8	£10	£15
Screed	£8	£10	£15
NOTE that lowest price assumes use of a full load of approximately 70 sq m. If only a small amount needed, the higher prices are applicable.			

TRADES YOU WILL NEED

BUILDER

For a 4.2x4.2m (14x14ft) room:
2 DAYS to remove the old floor and prepare the surface;
1 DAY to pour the floor;
1 DAY to lay the screed.

Laying a **concrete** floor is a **dirty and dusty** job, so make sure you **shield the rest of the house** as thoroughly as you can.

SEE BUILDERS p12–15 ▶

⌂ FLOORING

The type of flooring for a room must be selected with care. Whatever you choose will be staring you in the face for years, so you want to be sure it's the right thing.

CHOOSING A FLOOR One thing to consider is the floor covering in any adjacent rooms. Do you want the new floor covering to match it or provide a contrast? The purpose of the room will also affect your choice, as will the period and style of the rest of the house. Price is another consideration. When you are estimating the cost, take into account the cost of installation and any preparation, such as installing ply or screed over floorboards, underlay for carpets, junction strips and finishing or sealing the surface.

▶ **HARD FLOORS** are ideal for areas where there is heavy traffic, or where you want a finish that is easy to clean – such as in a bathroom or kitchen. Brick, concrete, stone, tiles or glass all offer hard-wearing solutions that are good to look at, age well and are long-lasting. They can feel cold or accentuate noise in the room, but that can be minimised by putting down rugs or by installing underfloor heating.

WOODEN FLOORS are another attractive and long-lasting solution. Wood is as fashionable today as it ever was and has a certain give that a hard floor lacks. It feels warm and ages beautifully but can be noisy – especially for people in the room below. Wood falls into two categories – hardwood and softwood. Pine and deal are both softwoods, less durable than hard and therefore cheaper. Hardwoods include ash, beech, maple and oak, the most commonly used in the home. Wood floors can be solid or a laminate, which has a thick veneer of real wood over a plywood base for strength. All wood should be seasoned so that it doesn't shrink or warp after it is laid (see Sanding floors, page 100) and, to my mind, should be from sustainable forests.

SHEET MATERIALS AND SOFT TILING are easy and quick to lay, providing a relatively cheap answer to flooring needs. There are both natural (lino and cork) and man-made (vinyl) options. If you care about the planet, steer away from the latter as its manufacture has the highest environmental impact. All of these are both lightweight and comfortable to walk on. Where these types of flooring score highly over some others is in terms of their easiness to clean. With the exception of cork, they also come in a staggering number of colours and designs.

➡ **CARPET** The mass production of carpet began in the eighteenth century, and the Industrial Revolution made it available to a much wider market. It is by far the softest, warmest and quietest way of covering a floor, and there is a huge variety to choose from. Originally carpet was made of 100% wool but today 80% wool is often mixed with 20% nylon, or perhaps another synthetic fibre such as polypropylene, to give better wear. There are also 100% synthetic carpets.

When choosing a carpet, you have to take into account what it is made of, the way it is made, the weight and density of the pile and what you will be using it for. It is not a good idea to use any kind of carpet in kitchens or bathrooms that are used a lot, because it can become dirty, damp and smelly.

CARPET IS USUALLY LABELLED AS:

➡ **HEAVY DOMESTIC** – For areas with heavy use, such as hallways and staircases.

➡ **MEDIUM TO HEAVY** – For family living rooms or studies.

➡ **MEDIUM TO LIGHT** – For living rooms.

➡ **LIGHT DOMESTIC** – For areas that get less use, such as bedrooms.

MATTING An alternative to wool carpeting, which offers the warmth and quiet without the softness, is a natural covering such as coir, seagrass or sisal. These provide a practical solution to suit almost any style of house. They are hard-wearing and attractive, and come in a range of different weaves and colours. These materials can be supplied in rolls to be cut and fitted like a carpet. Like carpet, they will need underlay installed before they are fitted. Before being laid professionally, they should be unrolled and left for 48 hours to adjust to the humidity of the room. However, natural coverings are very difficult to clean and have a tendency to shrink if they get damp, so they are unsuitable for use in areas such as bathrooms and kitchens.

With flooring, you generally get what you **pay** for. The **cheapest** solution will tend have the shortest life.

COST PER SQ M	£	££	£££
HARD FLOORS			
Brick pavers	£15	£20	£30
Concrete	£8	£10	£15
Stone	£18	£20	£45
Ceramic tiles	£20	£30	£45
Glass tiles	£20	£30	£45
WOOD, SHEET & TILES			
Wood block	£15	£27	£47
Wood laminate	£7	£10	£18
Parquet	£15	£27	£47
Lino	£15	£20	£25
Cork	£7	£18	£25
Vinyl sheet	£6	£15	£38
Vinyl tiles	£10	£30	£70
CARPET			
Carpet	£12	£33	£60
Nylon contract carpet	£2	£13	£50
Carpet tiles	£8	£20	£32

FLOOR COVERINGS	£	££	£££
MATTING			
Coir, per square metre	£10	£15	£25
Seagrass, per square metre	£10	£15	£25
Sisal, per square metre	£10	£15	£25

TRADES YOU WILL NEED

TILER	**2-3 DAYS**, to prepare, lay the tiles and grout a 4.2x4.2m (14x14ft) room.
FLOORING FITTER	**1 DAY**, for carpet or wood laminate. Allow an extra day if plywood or hardboard needs to be laid.
BRICKLAYER	**2-3 DAYS**, to lay a 4.2x4.2m (14x14ft) room.

SEE TILERS p32–33, **FLOORING FITTERS**, p36–37, **BRICKLAYERS** p18–19 ▶

SANDING FLOORS

More and more homes seem to be featuring hardwood flooring or exposed boards in preference to carpeting. If you are moving into an old property that still has the original boards, you may want to revive them. Originally all softwood was intended to be painted, so don't think you're restoring anything original by exposing it. That's not to say that you shouldn't do it, but don't view it as part of a great restoration process. If you are exposing boards on the first floor of a house, think about whether you want to install any insulation underneath them to dull the sounds of movement between that floor and the one below.

EXPOSING FLOORBOARDS Lift any existing carpet and look at the quality of the boards underneath. Check for and treat any signs of woodworm, wet or dry rot. If the majority of boards are in good condition, you will be able to get reclaimed boards to replace any missing, split or holed ones. The quality of reclaimed boards can vary enormously so hunt around for the most suitable ones. Don't expect the best reclaimed boards to come cheap. If you are fitting a parquet or wood block floor, remember that it has to be laid on screed or at least on a solid backing such as plywood.

PREPARATION Like any decorating job, the time taken for preparation is by far the most important part of the process. The room needs to be completely cleared and anything hanging on the wall removed in case the vibration of the sander dislodges anything. Boards may need to be replaced, nails that must be removed or punched in, old varnish or paint has to be sanded or removed, and gaps dealt with. Over a large area, it may be easier to close gaps by re-laying several boards closer together until you have a gap big enough to fit one new board. Otherwise, a mixture of sawdust and glue, or wooden fillets, can be inserted into narrow gaps.

SANDING Getting a smooth finish depends on three sandings with paper of an increasingly fine grain, usually by using a drum sander for the main area and an edging sander for the perimeter. This is a noisy and dirty job that will send a fine film of dust all over the house, so I recommend that you shut and tape up all doors.

FINISHING Once the boards are revealed in all their glory, there are number of suitable finishes – paint, stain and varnish, varnish wax. Paint and varnish need several coats, to make the floor as resistant as possible to wear and tear; you will probably need to redo it in about ten years. But in terms of maintenance, they have the edge over wax, which needs regular attention. If staining the wood, bear in mind that once it's done it can't be undone, whereas a coloured varnish can be changed.

Think twice about the floor varnish you use and beware of using water-based varnish. I have used varnishes that mark with water — this is really annoying when you've spent time and money on getting the look just right. I recommend that you get a professional sanding contractor to do this horrible, messy job. But messy as it is, it is well worth putting up with the inconvenience for the end result.

TRADES YOU WILL NEED

SANDING CONTRACTOR

2-3 days, for preparation of a double reception room and hall
(4.2 x 8.4m/14 x 28ft), depending on the state of the original boards;
1 day for sanding;
2 days for three coats of varnish by a specialist floor-sanding company.

FLOOR FINISHES	Coats	Durabilty	Maintenance
Wood stain	1-2	Can be waxed or sealed for tougher finish	LOW
Liming	1	Can be waxed or sealed for tougher finish	LOW
Polyurethane varnish	3	HIGH	LOW Just vacum/sweep and lightly mop
Water-based varnish	3	HIGH	MEDIUM Needs waxing 2–3 times a year
Paint	1-2	MEDIUM/LOW	EASY
Wax	1	HIGH	HIGH Needs regular reapplication
Oil	1-2	HIGH	MEDIUM Needs reapplication ever 1–2 years

NOTE Most varnishes come in gloss, semi-gloss, satin or matt finishes. They may darken the wood, so test a small patch first. Sanding should always follow the grain of the wood. Edges should be finished with an edge sander.

⌂ PARTITION WALLS

Before putting in a partition wall, think carefully about what the implications are for the two rooms on either side of it. Will you have to change the lighting? Is a door necessary? Will you need an extractor fan? Do you want to borrow light from the adjacent room by including a window or glass bricks? If you are making a bathroom or kitchen, think about where the units and plumbing will go in relation to the wall. It will probably be easier to run new pipes, wiring and sockets in the new wall than in the existing walls. Once you have thought the project through thoroughly, decide on the nature of the wall. Block walls or stud walls are the most commonly used, with steel framing gaining in popularity.

REGULATIONS Planning permission is not required for internal walls but they will have to satisfy building regulations with regard to fire safety, ventilation and drainage if you're installing a new kitchen or bathroom. There is a minimum in-built sound resistance required by building regulations. Discuss your plans with the Building Inspector, who will be able to advise you.

▶ **LIGHTWEIGHT BLOCK** walls are easily built, fireproof and provide good sound insulation. You will be able to fix units anywhere on the wall. They are usually used for internal ground floor or basement walls where load-bearing walls are needed.

▶ **STUD WALLS** are made from softwood with studs (verticals) at 400mm or 600mm intervals and noggins (cross bars) as required. Studwork is quick to do and cheaper than block walls. It is usually used for non-load-bearing walls. Plasterboard is screwed to the supports, then taped or skimmed. To increase sound insulation, use heavier boards and/or include insulation in the wall. Hollow walls are a good place for pipes and wiring. Plasterboard has no load-bearing ability, so units or shelves must be fixed to the studwork. Plan their position carefully first.

▶ **METAL FRAME** partition walls can be made from galvanised steel with studs 600mm apart. Because steel doesn't have the heat resistance of wood and will tend to buckle in extreme temperatures, it must be covered with one layer (30 minutes' resistance) or two layers (60 minutes') of fire-resistant board. Insulation, piping and wiring can easily be run within the wall. It offers a cheap and quick alternative to traditional studwork.

TRADES YOU WILL NEED

GENERAL BUILDER	**1 DAY**, for a general builder or a carpenter to install the studwork and dry-line it with plasterboard.
PLASTERER	**1 DAY** (although it will only take part of that day, you should expect to pay for a whole day).

PRICE PER SQ M	£
Internal blockwork	£15
Studwork partition	£20
Light steel partition	£5

You can **use the space** between the studwork as a very shallow **cupboard** accessed from one side – but you will be unable to insulate the wall.

SEE BUILDERS p12–15, **PLASTERERS** p28–29 ▶

⊕ PLASTERING AND DRY-LINING

Plastering is the traditional staging point between the first and second fixes. Once the structure of a building, and all the pipes and cables are in place, the walls are plastered to hide the sub-structure before plug socket cover plates, kitchen and bathroom units and other visible items are installed. Nowadays, dry-lining provides an alternative finish to wet plastering and is frequently used in new builds. Both finishes provide a surface ready for decoration. The question is which to choose.

▶ **WET PLASTER**, well skimmed, provides a great finish that you can simply have varnished, painted or papered over. Traditionally a mix of lime, sand and horsehair was used for the first coat, with neat lime as a second. Lime is still used today, but usually mixed in with sand and cement, when a breathable surface is required on a damp wall. Most plaster used internally is gypsum-based, with different additives that provide greater insulation or fire resistance, make the plaster more workable, or dry more slowly.

GYPSUM PLASTER should not be used on permanently damp walls because it will eventually crumble. Usually two coats of plaster, a render and set, are required for a good finish, although single-coat plasters are available. If it's an old house and you're trying to get an authentic finish, don't use metal anglebead. A good plasterer will be able to plaster in curves and around corners. The disadvantage of wet plaster is that it takes time to dry out thoroughly, so it is unwise to decorate too lavishly for six months or so – during which time slight cracks may appear (see Painting and Decorating, page 143).

It is advisable **not** to use **gypsum-based products** on the **inside of external walls** in any old building.

➡ **DRY-LINING** has the advantage of being relatively simple to do and avoids the drying-out period that plaster requires. Plasterboard comes in various types nailed, screwed or bonded to the walls and ceilings before being skimmed or decorated. However, I would always make sure it is screwed rather than nailed. In my experience, nails always pop out and once you've skimmed the surface, it's a frustrating and messy job to remove them. Alternatively, joints can be sealed and taped. Plasterboard can be foil-backed to inhibit damp; with high noise and heat insulation values; square-edged for plaster skimming (usually used on ceilings) or taper-edged for dry-lining. It comes in a variety of sizes and thicknesses, depending on the requirements of the job.

➡ **EXTERNAL RENDERING** is either used to protect a house in an exposed position or for its decorative effects. It can be flat and painted, pebbledashed, roughcast or with a Tyrolean finish. Remember to protect doors and windows while any of the last three are being put on. For straightforward rendering, it's advisable to always use sand, lime and cement render. Gypsum-based products should only be used on the interior of a building.

In any areas that are prone to damp, it's best to use a lime mortar because it allows moisture to pass through it.

If you're proposing to paint the rendered finish, make sure it can breathe and that the colour you choose harmonises with the other houses in the street. If you are living in a listed or leasehold building, there may be restrictions as to which colours can be used, so check beforehand.

PRICES

The price of plaster and plasterboard is negligible in comparison to the cost of the whole job. Generally a plasterer will supply materials and if not they will tell you the quantities they require so you can order them and get them delivered.

MATERIALS	£
Bag of gypsum plaster	£5
Sheet of plasterboard 2.4x1.2m (8x4ft)	£5

If you are buying plaster, **check its sell-by date.** Plaster only has a shelf life of about **3 months.**

TRADES YOU WILL NEED

PLASTERER

1 DAY, skimming a 4.2x4.2m (14x14ft) room.

SEE PLASTERERS p28–29 ▶

🏠 PUTTING IN NEW WINDOWS OR FRENCH DOORS

Apart from fulfilling the invaluable function of letting light into your house, windows and glazed doors are crucial to the appearance of the building. Their proportions make a massive difference to the look of the outside of the house. The question of whether to use timber or uPVC (unplasticised polyvinyl chloride) window frames arouses strong feelings.

▶ **TIMBER WINDOWS** Some favour timber frames because it is a natural, environmentally friendly material that lends character to a house. Manufactured frames come already treated with preservative and most are rebated so double glazing can be fitted. However, timber does need regular maintenance and repainting every five to ten years. Another disadvantage is that if a frame is badly made, it is liable to rot. If timber frames are properly maintained and well made there is no reason why they should not last for centuries.

▶ **UPVC WINDOWS** need little maintenance but do usually need to be replaced after about twenty-five years. They provoke criticism as their manufacture produces toxins that pollute the atmosphere.

▶ **METAL-FRAMED WINDOWS** were frequently used from the 1930s onwards but are rarely used today except in more commercial-style buildings.

WINDOW STYLES There are a number of standard styles to choose from, the most common being casement (opens on hinges) and sash (slides vertically) with single or multiple panes. Remember, the more panes you have, the more time-consuming they are to clean or paint. The most important thing, when replacing a window, is to respect the character and original design of the building itself.

REGULATIONS Since April 1, 2002, all new or replacement windows have had to meet the thermal insulation requirements of the building regulations. This is to prevent unnecessary energy loss. Today, windows must achieve a certain U-value (the lower the U-value, the lower the heat loss). If you are changing windows, this will almost certainly mean transferring from single-glazed windows to double-glazed windows. Additional insulation can be gained by using low-emissivity coated glass, or double-glazing where the gap is filled with an inert gas such as argon or xenon. Secondary glazing means keeping existing windows and fixing another layer of glass inside them. Less efficient than double-glazing, it can be made to fit or bought as ready-made units. Triple glazing is another possibility.

INSTALLATION Windows are generally fitted by the supplier although you could get a general builder or joiner to fit them. Any window installation must be done by a firm registered with FENSA (Fenestration Self-Assessment). Otherwise approval has to be obtained from your local authority, who must be satisfied that a window complies with building regulations. In the case of listed buildings or houses in conservation areas, check with your local planning office.

FRENCH DOORS: The correct term is 'French windows' but 'French doors' is more often used colloquially. As with windows, if installing or replacing French doors, do respect the character of your house, making sure that the doors suit it. Security is a priority with French doors. They should be fitted with rack bolts at both top and bottom.

➡️ **SLIDING PATIO DOORS** are a good alternative if you haven't got much space, or want a contemporary design.

WINDOWS	Number	£	££	£££
SASH WINDOWS				
UPVC		£200	£250	£400
Timber		£275	£350	£600
CASEMENT WINDOWS				
UPVC		£175	£200	£300
Timber		£225	£275	£350
Metal		£225	£275	£350
Hinges (pair)		£3	£4	£7
Handles		£5	£11	£25
WINDOW LOCKS				
Dual screws (pair)		£2	£3	£7
Sash stops (pair)		£3	£6	£11
Casement locks		£4	£5	£8
Cockspur handle		£5	£11	£25

FRENCH DOORS	Number	£	££	£££
Wood		£800	£1100	£1500
UPVC		£800	£1200	£1600
Hinges		£4	£7	£18
Handles		£12	£20	£45
Rack bolts		£8	£12	£15

Remember to fit window locks, especially on downstairs windows and small bathroom windows upstairs. Most insurance policies insist on this. There are locks to suit all different types of frames, so it's best to investigate when you buy the windows.

TRADES YOU WILL NEED

BUILDER

2 DAYS, to cut a hole for the window, fit the lintel and fix the doors/window in place.

PLASTERER

1 OR 2 DAYS, to make good.

SEE BUILDERS p12–15, **PLASTERERS** p28–29 ▶

⊕ HANGING INTERNAL DOORS

The easiest door to hang is a new one that precisely fits an accompanying new frame. It is much harder to make a door fit an existing frame. I would always get an experienced joiner to hang doors because if they are not hung perfectly, with everything in the right place, you end up with a door that will never shut properly. There are several kinds of door that can be used internally.

▶ **HOLLOW DOORS** consist of a wood fibre core sandwiched between two layers of board, with a solid lock block at the point where the handle is attached.

▶ **SOLID WOOD DOORS** are heavier and (unless they are very cheap) have a gratifying sturdiness. Softwood is generally painted or stained (depending on the quality of the wood) and used for most interior doors, while hardwood is reserved for doors that make a grand statement, as it is more expensive. Generally, new frame and panel doors are not supplied with ironmongery, so you will be able to choose your own.

RECLAIMED DOORS You can get old doors from a reclamation yard or reuse the existing doors in your house. Paint or strip and oil them, bearing in mind that if they are softwood, they would have originally been painted. There are companies that will take your doors away and dip them in baths of paint remover. I personally do not recommend this as soaking a door to this extent can sometimes make it warp and may dissolve the glue.

THERE ARE VARIOUS TYPES OF HINGES AVAILABLE FOR DOORS:

BUTT HINGES are most commonly used for hanging ordinary doors, and need a shallow recess cut in the door and the frame.

PROJECTING HINGES allow a door to swing back 180º, to lie against the wall.

PARLIAMENT HINGES also allow a door to swing 180º back against the wall but they have a smaller knuckle than a projecting hinge. Although these look better, they are weaker. If the internal door doubles as a fire door, check that the hinges have a fire certificate.

CHOOSING HINGES When choosing hinges, besides considering price and quality, think about the weight, height and thickness of the door. It is important that the hinge fits the door properly. When screwed to the door, it should either reach across the stile (vertical side) of the door completely, or leave at least 3mm (⅛in) showing. If you have fitted automatic door-closers, this adds 20% to the weight of the door. Does the finish of your chosen hinge (chrome, brass, aluminium, stainless steel, imitation bronze etc.) match that of the rest of the door furniture? Will the material you have selected rust? Check whether you need left- or right- handed hinges and be sure to buy the correct ones.

DOOR FURNITURE Different styles of door furniture are legion. Every style is available, from Louis XIV, Queen Anne and early Georgian to Regency, Victorian, Art Deco – and of course plenty of contemporary designs as well. Knobs or handles, locks and latches all have to be chosen. It's worth looking on the internet, or visiting a local ironmonger or good DIY store, to browse through the various options, taking the period and style of your house into account when choosing. Remember that a knob needs to be fitted with a longer latch than a handle, otherwise your knuckles can get scraped as the door opens.

DOOR SYSTEM Sometimes a door system is wanted that can be used to divide a large room occasionally without taking up too much space. Sliding doors are ideal if there's limited floor space, as furniture can be placed close to them. These use an upper track and floor-mounted guides that have to be installed. Bi-fold doors also work on a track and need less room to open than a regular door. Multi-fold doors work on a track and fold back until they are no wider than the wall. A potential disadvantage is that they are necessarily very thin, so provide little insulation. In my experience, cheap mechanisms never seem to work properly. It's worth spending that bit extra for a smooth operating system. The best option is to have a hollow wall so the door can slide back into it.

Use inexpensive flush fire doors and plant on an MDF sheet template to outline recessed panels and then detail with beading.

DOORS AND FITTINGS	£	££	£££
Hollow door	£18	£33	£40
Solid wood door	£25	£50	£70
Fire door	£25	£50	£90
Butt hinge	£2	£3	£6
Projecting hinge	£8	£15	£34
Parliament hinge	£8	£15	£34
Doorknob	£5	£16	£40
Door handle	£4	£20	£40
Folding door system, per metre	£8	£40	£120
Sliding door system, per metre	£8	£40	£120

TRADES YOU WILL NEED

CARPENTER

It should take about half a day to fit a door, but it's unlikely that a carpenter would charge for only half a day, so you really want to get him to hang two doors in a day.

SEE CARPENTERS p20–21 ▶

⊕ CHANGING BANISTERS OR A HANDRAIL

Apart from its obvious function, a staircase makes a great statement to anyone coming into a house. It immediately dictates the character of the house. Replacing it or moving it is a costly and complicated thing to do but changing the banisters or handrail can give an old staircase a new lease of life. Apart from the steps, the banisters are the key component of a staircase. They are made up of a handrail, a number of spindles or balusters joining it to the steps, and newel posts which secure the banister to the floor at the bottom of the flight of stairs and to the landings above.

BUILDING REGULATIONS require all staircases less than a metre wide to have one handrail. Any wider, and they must have two. Some people choose to remove their banisters, but this is contrary to building regulations. If you have an an additional handrail attached to the wall, make sure that it is very securely attached to prevent any accidents.

NEWEL POSTS are part of the integral structure of a staircase and so are more difficult to change than the spindles. To do so would probably involve dismantling the staircase altogether. Alternatively, you can slice the post off at the bottom, but this will significantly weaken the banister. Try to avoid changing the post.

SPINDLES Grand, old houses had ornate staircases with turned spindles and newel posts. These were sometimes replaced with simple straight spindles, or even boarded in. Today there are many decorative machine-turned styles to choose from. They are either housed in, sub-tenoned or nailed to the underside of the handrail and the top of the steps or the closed string (the panel that closes in the ends of the treads). Try to pick spindles that suit the character and period of your home.

HANDRAILS are available in hard or softwood, steel, brass, glass and more, in numerous styles. Let the house dictate your choice.

CONTEMPORARY BANISTERS Nowadays, sheet glass or metal can be used in a contemporary application. These vary massively in cost and you will need to price them individually with either a staircase designer, metal fabricator or glazier.

A **staircase** dictates the **character** of the **house!**

STAIRCASE	£	££	£££
Plain wooden spindles	£2	£4	£5
Turned wooden spindles	£4	£12	£25
Wooden handrail per metre	£5	£13	£25
Metal handrail per metre	£15	£25	£40
Wooden newel post	£13	£20	£30

TRADES YOU WILL NEED

CARPENTER

2 DAYS, to change the spindles and handrail. If the newel posts are to be changed it is a major job, which will take longer.

SEE CARPENTERS p20–21 ▶

# REWIRING

NICEIC (National Inspection Council for Electrical Installation Contracting) recommends that electrical systems should be checked every ten years. If there are cables in black rubber, lead or fabric, or an archaic fusebox, cast-iron switches, round-pin sockets, round switches, braided flex, no earthing — it's definitely time that the house was rewired.

REGULATIONS As of January 2005, new safety regulations demand that if you are thinking of doing any major electrical work you must get the local authority's building control involved. Sockets must be no lower than 450mm from the floor and switches must not be higher than 1200mm. Minor jobs like replacing a socket front or light switch are not affected. Rewiring a house while living in it can be done with relatively little disruption if you have a good electrician. All work must qualify for a minor works certificate, which your electrician will give you after the system has been tested. This confirms that the work has been 'designed, constructed, inspected, tested and verified in accordance with the national standard for the safety of electrical installations'. Without it, your house insurance may become invalid and it may be difficult to sell your home.

SEE ELECTRICIANS p26–27 ▶

PLANNING THE ELECTRICAL LAYOUT

Go through each room, working out all the possible permutations and marking where you want the sockets, switches and lights so your electrician can install the right number of circuits.

A KITCHEN LIGHTING PLAN

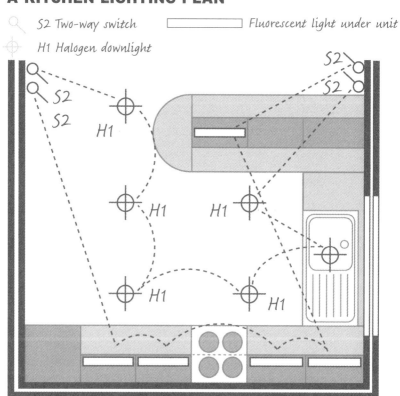

S2 Two-way switch   Fluorescent light under unit

H1 Halogen downlight

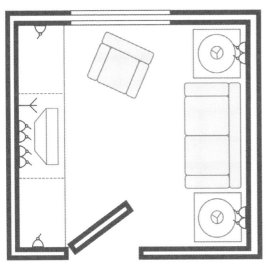

LIVING ROOM SOCKET LAYOUT

⌂ Switched socket

⌂⌂ Double switched socket

Y Aerial

A BATHROOM LIGHTING PLAN

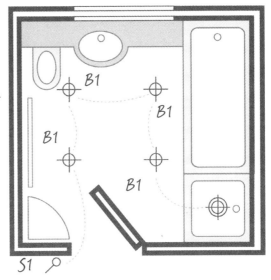

⚲ S1 Single switch

⊕ B1 Zone 2 downlight

⊕ Downlight and extractor

CABLES In a full restoration, most of the time involved in wiring a house consists of running the cables and chasing them in – known as the first fix. If you surface-mount the wires, it's much cheaper but it generally looks pretty awful unless you're going for a utilitarian design using round conduit (tube). I would try and avoid plastic casing unless it's in your garden shed!

THERE ARE VARIOUS TYPES OF LIGHTING USED IN THE HOUSE:

▶ **AMBIENT** – For atmosphere. Usually wall lights, downlighters, uplighters or pendant lights.

▶ **TASK** – For illuminating areas used for work. Usually spotlights, downlighters, directional tracking, single table lamps.

▶ **ACCENT** – For highlighting particular features. Usually spotlights, directional tracking, downlighters and uplighters.

PLANNING The key to wiring is to plan it, plan it and plan it again. Think about exactly how you will be using each room as well as how you might use it differently in the future. Will a dining room or spare bedroom double as a study? Where will the children do their homework? Might you move the television or sound system? If you want wall-mounted lights, either for ambient light or for accenting pictures, it is best to wire them in during the first fix.

SPECIAL AREAS Make sure that any areas where you will be working (for instance the kitchen – particularly over worktops – or a study) or reading (by the bed or in the sitting room) are adequately lit. Do you want lighting under the wall units in the kitchen to light the worktop? Do you want ceiling downlighters anywhere, (usually most easily installed from the floor above)? Think about mirrors, particularly in the bathroom, and make sure they are well lit.

SWITCHING Bear in mind where you will switch lights on and off. For instance, if you enter and exit a room through two different doors, include two-way switches at each (remembering that you will pay more for the extra cable runs). Do you want all or some of the lights to be switched through one switch, or do you want individual switches for some or all of them? Bathroom lighting will have to be switched from outside the room. At what level on the wall do you want the switches positioned? Do you want to use dimmer switches anywhere?

OTHER EQUIPMENT Also remember telephone points, TV aerials, computer connections, entertainment systems, smoke and burglar alarms – all these wires can be hidden during the first fix. What you don't want to have to do is to add a socket later on. If in any doubt at the planning stage, put one in. It's better to have extra sockets that you don't use than cables snaking across the floor. Make sure you have deep back boxes or you lose the option to have flush socket fronts. It's an effort to go back and redo them later.

TRADES YOU WILL NEED

ELECTRICIAN

ABOUT 2 WEEKS, to do a basic rewire of a 3-bed house (empty site), and finish ready for decoration.

1–2 DAYS, to add an extra socket or light depending on the cable run.

1 DAY, to fit a new consumer unit (fuse box). It must use MCBs (miniature circuit-breakers) not old-fashioned re-wireable fuses.

SEE ELECTRICIAN p26–27 ▶

FITTINGS	£	££	£££
SOCKETS			
Single sockets	£3	£5	£8
Double sockets	£6	£10	£15
SWITCH PLATES			
Plastic single 1-way	£1	£2	£4
Metal single 1-way	£8	£10	£20
Clear single 1-way	£3	£4	£6
Dimmer single 1-way	£5	£6	£10
Plastic single 2-way	£2	£4	£7
Plastic double 2-way	£3	£5	£10
LIGHT FITTINGS			
Recessed downlight	£2	£4	£10
Mains (240V) halogen downlight	£2	£4	£8
Transformer (110V) downlight	£3	£7	£10
Ceiling rose and bulb fitting	£4	£6	£7
Pendant light fitting	£25	£150	£250
Wall light	£15	£40	£100

⊕ NEW BOILER

An efficient boiler will provide a house with hot water and heating in the most economical way. Those days of high heating bills and of irritation from showers that turn freezing cold when another tap in the house is turned on will vanish. The Energy Savings Trust suggests that an average boiler has a life of about fifteen years, but in my experience many don't last that long. After that, it's time to think about changing it. Once you have chosen whether you prefer a gas- or oil-fired system, consider whether the boiler will be heating the house or just the hot water (i.e. to use night storage heaters). The next consideration is what kind of boiler you want.

▶ **TRADITIONAL BOILER** This type of boiler heats water and stores it in a tank.

▶ **COMBINATION BOILER** This heats water direct from the mains on demand, without requiring a storage tank. The combination boiler also provides heating. You can use a hot water cylinder, and therefore an immersion heater as well, with a combination boiler if you want more hot water.

REGULATIONS New boilers must be 'high efficiency' and generally this will mean a condensing boiler. As of April 2005, new government regulations demand that all new boilers reach a Seasonal Efficiency of Domestic Boilers in the UK (SEDBUK) A or B rating. A condensing boiler uses 30–40% less fuel thanks to an extra heat exchanger, which removes the heat from the burning fuel and condenses liquid in the flue to be drained away, so saving on fuel, cost and carbon emissions. This is without doubt a more environmentally friendly option.

POSITIONING THE BOILER The best place to site a boiler is near to the places where hot water is used most – such as the bathroom or shower room, or next to the washing machine or dishwasher. If you live in an area that has hard water, ask your installer or supplier whether to add a liquid anti-limescale product to the system, and put a scale inhibitor on the cold-water feed to either the boiler or to the house itself.

New boilers must be 'high efficiency'!

BOILERS	£	££	£££
High-efficiency standard boiler	£800	£1,300	£1,900
High-efficiency combination boiler	£600	£1,800	£2,500

Double-check that the boiler is the right one for your home. **Oversized boilers** run less efficiently and **cost more** to buy. Your supplier should be able to advise you.

TRADES YOU WILL NEED

PLUMBER

1 DAY, for replacing the same type of system, if it is in the same location. He must be registered by CORGI or OFTEC, depending whether the boiler is gas or oil powered.

SEE PLUMBERS p24–25 ▶

⌂ NEW CENTRAL HEATING

Changing your boiler may be enough to give an improvement in an old central heating system, but it may not solve the problem. If this is the case, you need to look at the other elements that make up the heating system.

RADIATORS have varying lifespans. When they approach the end of their life, the welded seams start to rust and tend to weep. That's when it's probably easier to simply replace them. Over the years, sludge can build up inside making them work less efficiently. The system can be flushed through, but it isn't always enough. Another reason to replace is for aesthetic reasons − when the style of the radiator doesn't suit the style of room that you are trying to create.

PIPEWORK Old central heating systems used steel piping, which sucked heat from the water and meant that the system needed to circulate much hotter water than a system with copper piping. Copper has the advantage of being non-toxic, non-corrosive and relatively easy to bend and install.

However, there are also a number of reasons to replace copper pipework – if the system is badly organised, doesn't function as efficiently as it should, or won't accommodate any more radiators when you want. Pipes laid by a good plumber will look like a work of art, running parallel, with all the corners turning at the same point. A bodged job will have pipes running all over the place as the plumber hoped for the best. Remember the greatest cost of running new central heating will be lifting and replacing the floorboards throughout the house and fitting the pipework.

PIPE DIMENSIONS In older houses the pipework will be measured in inches, but it is important to remember that this measurement refers to the INNER diameter of the pipe, whereas the current metric system refers to the OUTER diameter. Copper pipework is normally 15mm or ½in for the carcassing around the house. If you have a big house, you may want to run the main ring in a bigger pipe so more water gets round faster. Common dimensions are: 8mm and 10mm – for microbore central heating systems ;12mm and 15mm – for connections to individual taps, appliances etc.; 22mm, 28mm and 35mm – for long runs where use of 15mm piping would cause too much of a pressure drop.

UNDERFLOOR HEATING Instead of conventional central heating with radiators that can get in the way, some people prefer underfloor heating. I'm not a great fan because you can't heat a room up and cool it down quickly. But the constant temperature means it can be great in a bathroom. Underfloor heating systems vary but they are all inexpensive to install (on an empty site), will fit under any kind of flooring and are economical to run.

Using radiator valves

(ideally thermostatic) on a radiator means you can **control the temperature** in that particular room. For instance in a spare room that isn't constantly being used, you can turn the valve to zero so the **hot water** only runs through the pipework without going through the radiator. When you want to **heat the room**, all you have to do is **turn the valve up**.

PRICES

To run the central heating pipework you need to buy the right fittings and plan the job very well, therefore, in my opinion, it is best to ask the plumber to supply them. The choice of radiators is more difficult. If you want to get away from the standard convector radiator, there are reconditioned old radiators or a choice of modern radiators designed to make a statement.

RADIATOR	£	££	£££
300x400mm (HxW)			
Standard	£15	£25	£40
Designer	£200	£500	£1,000
Old school	£270	£350	£500
700x3,000mm (HxW)			
Standard	£35	£55	£120
Designer	£500	£1,500	£3,000
Old school	£500	£700	£1,000
Underfloor heating system (per square metre)	£200	£400	£650

The greatest cost will be lifting and replacing the floorboards!

TRADES YOU WILL NEED

PLUMBER	
🛁🛁🛁🛁 🛁🛁🛁	**ABOUT 7 DAYS**, to set up a standard three-bedroom house, if the site is empty.
🛁🛁🛁🛁 🛁🛁🛁	**7 DAYS**, to fit the entire system throughout the house.
🛁🛁	**2 DAYS**, to fit the radiators.
🛁	**1 DAY**, to fill and test the system.
🛁	**1 DAY**, to install the boiler.

SEE PLUMBERS p24–25 ▶

⬣ BUILDING CUPBOARDS

The key to a 'designer home' is a clutter-free space. The only way to achieve that space, apart from throwing everything away, is to have plenty of storage.

➤ **FREESTANDING STORAGE** Don't automatically build fitted cupboards. Think about buying a beautiful wardrobe to fit into a space in the bedroom or even in the living room. While building cupboards is the most economic use of a space, spanning the distance wall to wall, I prefer freestanding cupboards if the room is big enough. An antique wardrobe can make a good feature in a room.

➤ **BUILT-IN STORAGE** If your space is limited, built-in cupboards are the best solution. Those in regular use should be easily accessible and positioned roughly between hip and eye level. You don't want to have to drag out a ladder each time you need a pair of socks or be continuously bending or reaching for things you often use in the kitchen. If you want a cupboard to house heavy things, put it low down so that you don't break your back getting things out or putting them away. If you're building a wardrobe, it's worth having part of it fitted with two hanging rails for shirts and trousers. You don't need full height for either.

PLANNING Think about putting cupboards in places you wouldn't normally expect to find them. I have seen drawers built into the risers of a staircase; I have also see a cupboard built into the studwork on some stairs. It was only about 75mm (3in) deep but it was perfect for kitchen things like spices. If you have internal folding wooden shutters, there is sometimes room in the recess for a cupboard big enough to hold tapes, CDs and DVDs. What about over the top of a door? What about over a fitted wardrobe? That high-up dead space is ideal for storing things you rarely use.

MATERIALS Don't scrimp and save on hinges or on wood for the doors. The carcass can be cheaply built but the door should clunk shut solidly. Many cupboards are made of MDF but cut it in a well-ventilated room and use breathing apparatus – the dust is bad for your health. The great thing about MDF is that it comes in different widths and takes paint well so you're assured of a good finish.

STORAGE	£	££	£££
Freestanding tall cupboard	£60	£250	£400
Freestanding low cupboard	£50	£200	£350
Freestanding chest of drawers	£45	£250	£500
Built in tall cupboard per metre	£300	£500	£700
Built in low cupboard per metre	£200	£350	£400

Make use of **forgotten dead space!**

TRADES YOU WILL NEED

CARPENTER/ JOINER

Obviously the carpenter's time depends on the size of the cupboard built. However, wardrobes either side of an alcove with a top cupboard and hanging space underneath would take about 5 days to build and fit, and 4 days to decorate.

SEE CARPENTERS/JOINERS p20–21 ▶

🏠 DECORATING A ROOM

Anyone can splash a bit of paint around a room, but the secret of a really good decorating job is all in the preparation. I can't emphasise enough how important it is. A decorator's job is 80% preparation. Changing the colour of a room is a very different job to decorating a room where there has been major building work.

PREPARATION The room should be as empty and clean as possible. Protect the floor with dustsheets and mask the perimeter with tape to ensure it doesn't get paint on it by mistake. New plaster must be allowed to dry out properly (ideally for six months) before painting, unless you're opting for non-vinyl paint. Otherwise, shrinkage cracks appear, and making good and redecorating could be a costly and frustrating business. The only way of preventing cracks is by letting it dry incredibly slowly. If cracks do appear, rake them out with a screwdriver until you have a proper hole you can fill.

In a new room, the decorator has to make good after work done by the other tradesmen, finishing around the holes cut by the electrician and plumber, and filling any holes in woodwork that the carpenter may have left. All timber has to be properly knotted and primed. A primer seals the wood and makes a base for other coats of paint. Knotting stops resin leaking out of knots and discolouring paintwork, while primer seals wood and makes a base for other coats of paint. Don't think it doesn't matter because you're having the skirting, doors and window frames painted. If you don't knot and prime, you'll pay the price. Skirting boards or architraves should have been primed or undercoated before being fixed in place. If you scrimp and save the preparation, it will show in the finish.

REDECORATING If a room is to be redecorated, all wallpaper should be completely stripped off and removed unless it is sound enough to paint over. The walls will need thoroughly rubbing down, sanding and making good. This can take several days, depending on the size of the room.

WINDOWS When painting, cut in windows properly, to form a seal between the glass and the woodwork. This can be fiddly, especially on a multi-paned window. Some people use masking tape, but to get a good seal it is better avoided.

PAINT Good-quality paint will generally provide better coverage and last much longer than a cheaper brand. Again, scrimping and saving on the paint will show in the results. Make sure you specify the particular paint you want at the start, so the decorator can allow for it in his estimate. For every job there is a different type: matt, gloss or eggshell for woodwork, depending on the level of sheen you want; matt emulsion, or vinyl silk emulsion with a slight sheen, for interior walls. There is also one-coat paint, non-drip paint, water-based paint, solvent-based paint – in fact a bewildering array of different choices. Take advice from a decorating supplier, or ask your decorator for his recommendation, if you are unsure which is the best type for the job in hand.

If you use **masking tape** to mask off floors and windows, remove it within 24 hours or the **glue will harden** and it will become a nightmare to remove!

PAINT QUANTITIES	*Coverage*
Coverage per litre based on one coat of paint	
INTERIOR WALLS AND CEILINGS	
Matt emulsion	up to 13 sq m
Silk	up to 13 sq m
INTERIOR WOOD AND METAL	
Eggshell	up to 17 sq m
Gloss	up to 18 sq m
Satinwood	up to 17 sq m
EXTERIOR ITEMS	
Smooth wall	up to 15 sq m
Textured wall	up to 8 sq m
Exterior gloss for wood and metal	up to 18 sq m

BASIC PAINT QUANTITY FOR ONE COAT

Total area of each wall is width multiplied by height

(4.2x2.5m = 10.50 sq m/14x8ft = 112 sq ft)

To calculate the amount of paint required for a whole room, add the quantity for each wall together.

MATERIALS	£
Oil-based paint for woodwork per litre	£10
Water-based paint for walls/ceilings per litre	£6
Lining paper, per roll	£3
Wallpaper, per roll	£10

80% of a decorating job is **preparation!**

TRADES YOU WILL NEED

DECORATOR

1 DAY TO 2 WEEKS, depending on how well you want it done, to decorate a standard 4.2x4.2m (14x14ft) room.

I tell my decorator what sort of job I want done, from a 'tosh and splosh', to a really perfect finish, which determines how long the job takes.

SEE DECORATORS p34–35 ▶

🏠 NEW FRONT DOOR

When choosing a new front door, make sure you go for a style that is appropriate for the building. So either select a door that fits the period of the original architecture of the house, or something contemporary. Look at your neighbours' doors and if possible choose something that will fit with the look of the street.

▶ **HARDWOOD DOORS** These were traditionally waxed and sealed because oak, the most commonly grown British hardwood, does not take well to being painted – unlike utile, another hardwood, which was imported.

▶ **SOFTWOOD DOORS** These were generally painted the same colour as the rest of the external woodwork. During the second half of the eighteenth century, front doors were usually painted in black, dark green, brown or grey gloss. During the Edwardian era, the full gamut of colours began to be used outside, sometimes with contrasting colours on the frame, the panels or their bevelled edges.

There was quite a range of styles to choose from. Some doors had panels that were raised and fielded (bevelled) and some had panels in glass, either etched or stained for privacy, to let light into the dingy halls behind them.

▶ **RECLAIMED DOORS** If you are looking for a reclaimed door, head off to the local architectural salvage yard. Beware – old doors come in all sorts of shapes and sizes and may not fit into a modern standard-sized doorframe. Doors can generally be handmade to fit by a joiner or carpenter. Otherwise you will find a massive choice at a local builder's merchant or DIY store.

▶ **UPVC** There is a vast array of styles and finishes of UPVC front doors. For security reasons, choose a door with a key entry system, not one that depends on a lever or handle. These doors aren't strong enough to have extra locks or bolts fitted, but should come with in-built deadlock, shoot bolts or a multi-point locking system. Think also about a weatherproof seal around the door.

SECURITY You will want to add modern security devices to your front door. A peephole at eye level allows you to see who is on the other side before you open up. A chain lets you open just a little way. A front door needs strong locks and bolts, such as a mortise or cylinder rim lock securing it from the outside, with rack bolts or hinge bolts on the inside. Some companies supply locks where you have to produce the house title deeds and your passport and go to central London to get a new key. Think twice about this unless you're prepared to take an entire day off each time. Also remember that laminated glass is more resistant than toughened glass.

DOOR FURNITURE is another consideration. Again, make sure the hinges, handle, door knocker and letterbox are consistent and match the style of door. Victorian-style furniture on a Georgian-style door can look a little odd. Letterbox plates can be fitted horizontally or vertically. When you choose one, take into account the amount and type of mail you get. If you are likely to get a lot of packages, a large letter plate will avoid trips to the Post Office to pick up things the postman hasn't been able to deliver. Similarly, think about whether you would like a mesh letterbox or a draught-excluding flap on the inside.

UNIT	Number	£	££	£££
Hardwood door		£175	£250	£350
Softwood door		£60	£160	£260
UPVC (includes furniture)		£200	£400	£750
Doorknob		£5	£20	£44
Door handle		£6	£20	£25
Door knocker		£13	£25	£55
Letterbox		£4	£10	£22
Peephole		£2	£3	£15
Chain bolt		£2	£3	£19
Mortise lock		£9	£13	£33
Cylinder rim lock		£6	£9	£30

TRADES YOU WILL NEED

JOINER

1 DAY. (Also 2 days for a decorator if the door needs painting.)

SEE JOINERS p20–21 ▶

🏠 DAMP AND PESTS

There are lots of damp and pest problems that can afflict a house but the most common of these are rising damp, wet and dry rot, and woodworm.

▶ **RISING DAMP** is one of the most common scares. Remember: your house will NOT fall down. Yes, you'll have wet walls but there's no need to panic. Rising damp is often confused with condensation, which is caused by inadequate ventilation, causing the external walls to become saturated. The ground level outside the house should be at least 150mm (6in) lower than the inside ground level. If it is higher, that is often a cause of rising damp. One solution is to dig a trench around the outside of the house and put shingle in the bottom, thus lowering the ground level immediately next to the house. Sometimes damp is caused when the external render covers the damp-proof course. A simple remedy is to hack off the render. Many old houses weren't built with damp-proof courses. The injection of a damp-proof course into a wall is meant to form a horizontal damp-proof course although it doesn't always work. You can hack off internal render and replaster yourself, asking a plasterer to make good, but remember a guarantee will often only be given if a damp-proofing company does the lot.

Leaking guttering is one of the most common causes of rot. Keep gutters clear. Next time it's raining, go outside and look at yours, to make sure water isn't running down the outside of the house.

▶ **PENETRATING DAMP** can be caused by leaking or blocked downpipe or gutters, cracked brickwork or tiles, archaic pointing, old, porous bricks — to name but a few. All of these problems can be remedied by you or your builder. Damp may even be caused by something as obvious as water splashed up by cars driving past. Traditionally, lime mortar was used for external rendering and internal plastering (see Plastering and drylining, page 107). Today, you should mix in a waterproof additive into a render of lime and cement.

DRY ROT should be taken seriously. It can cause wide-ranging destruction if left unchecked. If you don't spot the rot itself or see evidence of cracked wood, you may become aware of its strong fungal smell. Dry rot needs moisture to survive and will seek it out for itself. If there is a dark, warm, unventilated damp place, it may well take hold before it is noticed. There will be a main fruiting body, like a flattish mushroom, which throws out ginger spores, that will develop into more fruiting bodies with white tendrils or mycelia that travel across woodwork or masonry. Sometimes you may see white cotton-wool-like growths. The mycelia suck the moisture out of the wood, making it crack across the grain and lose its structural integrity. It can travel a long way behind plaster without being seen on the surface. If the rot is not dealt with, eventually all wood in the house will disintegrate entirely. The source of the moisture needs to be removed and the main fruiting body and the mycelia must be exposed and killed. It is recommended that the affected area should be cut out to at least a metre beyond the last visible sign and then the whole area treated with fungicide. All damaged timber will have to be replaced with treated timber, and sound original timber treated also.

WET ROT is found in damp timber. If windows or doors are neglected or badly made (particularly the area around the joints), water will make its way in and the timber will begin to deteriorate. Watch for peeling paintwork and spongy, disintegrating or splitting woodwork. Don't panic but treat it as soon as possible. Work out the source of the moisture and remove it. All the decayed wood should be removed and a new piece of wood spliced in, then filled and repainted. If very badly rotted, replace the whole piece of damaged timber. Unlike dry rot, which seeks out moisture, wet rot has to have moisture supplied.

WOODWORM The most frequent of all pests is woodworm. Many old houses have had woodworm at some stage. The sign of an active attack is a rash of small holes in timber with wood dust present, where the insects have bored their way through. Fortunately, it's a relatively simple procedure to treat it. A small outbreak can be treated with an insecticide sprayed or squirted into the affected area. If the attack is more serious, a specialist contractor will need to come and spray under the floorboards and the roof timbers. Be aware that if you have a floor sanded only a few days after spraying the top against woodworm, the chemicals will be sanded off too. You really need to lift every few boards and spray underneath.

ACTION There's a lot of scaremongering about these problems and huge prices are quoted to solve them. Sit down and think logically about the situation and don't panic.

Depending on the problem, you will need different tradesmen. They may include a carpenter, plasterer and general builder. There are specialist companies who will charge you for a damp and timber survey, telling you where they suggest remedial work should be carried out. If you appoint them to do the job, the cost of this is then taken off the cost of the work. You may find, though, that the price of the work is rather more expensive through one of these specialist companies than through a smaller contractor – although you will get a guarantee which, if you come to sell the house, may give the new buyers some element of comfort.

Save money by lifting up the carpets and the floorboards yourself!

TRADES YOU WILL NEED

GENERAL BUILDER

1–5 DAYS, depending on where and what the problem, a general builder should be able to deal effectively with minor outbreaks.

CONTRACTOR

1–10 DAYS, depending on the scale of the problem. A contractor will be able to call on tradesmen as he needs them. They may include a builder to remove affected areas, a carpenter to replace woodwork, and a plasterer to make good.

SPECIALIST COMPANY

2–7 DAYS. A specialist company has have all the equipment and manpower to deal with large outbreaks quickly. It should also offer a guarantee against the problem reappearing.

SEE BUILDERS p12 – 15 ▶

⌂ FIRE PREVENTION

All new building work has to comply with building regulations that include strict fire safety regulations. These are to enable you and your family get out of the house unhurt in the event of a fire.

ALARM SYSTEMS If you are doing any work that is subject to building regulations, you will need to comply with fire protection regulations. However, it is sensible for all buildings to be equipped with smoke alarms or fire detection and alarm systems. The regulations specify which system is required for different types of building. All houses should have a system connected to the mains electricity system, with a battery-operated back-up system. Alarms should be placed between bedrooms and in places where fires are most likely to start i.e. in kitchens and living rooms. There should be a smoke detector within 3m (10ft) of each bedroom door. There should be at least one alarm on each storey. The system should be interconnected so that when when one alarm goes off, it triggers the others in the house. Again there are precise requirements about the location and maintenance of the alarms.

SMOKE DETECTORS There is more than one type of detector to choose from that complies with the regulations. Ionisation alarms detect all invisible smoke particles so respond quickly to flames from something like a burning chip pan. Optical alarms respond to all smoke, but are particularly reactive to large particles in the smoke from smouldering objects such as burning furniture. Heat sensors get triggered by heat and are particularly useful in a kitchen. It is possible to use a combination of these detectors on one system.

Don't try and save costs. If you're doing any building work at all, bite the bullet and put in smoke detectors. They are obligatory in all rental flats and new builds.

ESCAPE ROUTES Building regulations tell you where you need a protected escape route – again only if you are doing building work. Providing this in a one- or two-storey house is quite easy. Each room should have a window that will open enough for you to be able to escape (building regulations are quite specific about dimensions and position) or, with the exception of the kitchen, open to a hall leading to the exit. If you have window locks, keep a key close to the window. Basements should have a protected stairway to the floor above or a window or door to escape through. The regulations are precise about which rooms – kitchens, utility rooms, dressing rooms, bathrooms – can only be reached through another room.

NEW BUILD For all new houses (built since 1992) with more than two storeys, defined as over 4.5m high, building regulations require a protected escape route from the upper floors. This means that the walls surrounding it must be able to resist fire for at least thirty minutes and the doors for twenty minutes. Most untreated old or reclaimed wooden doors don't comply. It may be possible to upgrade them by using fireproof paints, depending on their condition. Fire doors must be appropriately sealed and have smoke seals fitted. There are also required standards for glazed doors. All fire doors must be fitted with automatic closers. If you are adding a loft extension to an old house, the exit route will have to comply with the above. This may involve you in extra unbudgeted expense.

If in any doubt, consult your local Building Inspector.

ALARM SYSTEMS	£	£££
Ionisation alarm system for 3-bed house	£1,000	£5,000
Optical alarm system for 3-bed house	£1,000	£5,000
NOTE both are often installed as part of burglar alarm system		

Consider investing in a **fire extinguisher** and/or **fire blankets** in kitchen and living room – where fires are most likely to start.

TRADES YOU WILL NEED

ELECTRICIAN

1 DAY, to fit the fire alarm system (depending on the size of house and the number of alarms needed).

SEE ELECTRICIANS p26–27 ▶

⊙ RE-ROOFING

Natural materials such as – tiles, slate, straw, stone or shingles make fantastic roof coverings. All of them are long-lived (except straw – reed thatch should last for 25 years if netted) and weather attractively, but eventually they will need replacing. Plants such as ivy, moss, wisteria or Virginia creeper might look great growing over a roof but can do lasting damage. Sometimes, over time, roof timbers may be damaged, become infested with insects or rot if water has been prevented from flowing off the roof freely.

▶ **SLATE** There are slate quarries all over the world and some types of slate have a longer life than others. The colour of slate varies according to the region – rusty brown and grey from Cornwall, greens from Westmoreland. The slate most commonly used in the UK is Welsh slate, a familiar bluey grey, that can be split quite thinly. One way to test the quality of slate is to see if it rings well when tapped with another slate, which means it is solid – if it is not, it is probably shot. Another test is to see how slates break – if they break in a weak and powdery way, they are past their lifespan and probably most of the roof is too, but if it breaks cleanly then they can all generally be reused.

➡ TILES Beware of replacing slate with tiles. Tiles are heavier so the roof may have to be modified and supported. This will need to comply with building regulations. I strongly suggest that you replace a roof with like for like. It will look much better too. If you are only replacing part of a roof, try to match the original slates or tiles as closely as possible. Bear in mind that second-hand reclaimed slates and tiles can be more expensive than new and they don't come with a guarantee.

CHOOSING A ROOFER This is the one job you should never get done on day rates. Always get two or three prices for the whole job from different companies. But don't just go on price, go and look at the roofers' last job as well. A badly finished roof looks terrible and won't last – and may well leak. Look at the detail and the way they have finished it all off, including the lead flashings, cement fillets and edges.

Some roofers will work incredibly fast but, quite reasonably, will be charging the same overall amount for the work as someone who does the same job much slower. Remember, a roofer's work is seasonal. In fine, clear weather they'll be all over the roof like ants and when it's pouring down with rain they'll often be sitting around drinking tea.

ROOFING is an art in itself. After stripping the existing roof, roofers use a breathable waterproof membrane often known as 'felt'. It usually comes on a roll so is easy to roll out. Then it is secured in place using wooden battens which should have been treated to withstand rot and insect attack. Then the slates or tiles are nailed to the battens.

LOFT INSULATION Loft insulation is simple to install and makes an enormous difference to the heat loss from a house. It comes as rolls of fibreglass which are rolled out between the joists. Beware of the glass fibres which stick into the skin and are very itchy. Use protective clothing when handling it and if you do get it on your skin wash it off in a cold shower to stop the pores opening up as you wash the fibres off. Always wear a dust mask. Sheet wool is a more expensive option, but is also more environmentally friendly.

PLANNING PERMISSION is generally needed if you are extending a roof. Listed building permission may also be necessary if you are changing the roof covering or making any changes to the front face of the roof such as adding roof lights. There are no building regulations for re-roofing ordinary property if you are simply re-roofing.

RE-ROOFING	Number	£	££	£££
One slate		£15	£35	£65
One tile		£8	£12	£15
NOTE prices depend very much on the total order quantity				
Re-roof 3-bed house with slates		£6,500	£8,000	£11,000
Re-roof 3-bed house with tiles		£5,000	£6,000	£8,000

Choose a roofer by the quality of his work!

TRADES YOU WILL NEED

ROOFER

A 3-bedroom house CAN be roofed in only 5 days.

Scaffolding for front only of 3-bed house is £400 for 4 weeks and £50 per week after that.

SEE ROOFERS p22–23 ▶

⌂ NEW GUTTERING AND FASCIA

Traditionally, guttering and drainpipes were made in cast iron or even, sometimes, lead. The disadvantages of these are that they are heavy, need painting, might rust and are liable to crack or split.

▶ **CAST ALUMINIUM** is lighter than cast iron and is generally pre-painted.

▶ **ROLLED SHEET ALUMINIUM** will not corrode and can be painted if desired.

▶ **PLASTIC** is used almost universally. Some people prefer cast iron rainwear for its looks, particularly on historic buildings. In time, plastic guttering frequently leaks at the joints, but that is usually straightforward to fix. This is far outweighed by the benefits of longevity, ease of maintenance and lack of weight. If you are only replacing part of the guttering or some of the downpipes, match the material to the original. Mixing plastic with cast iron can look messy.

GUTTERING There are three types of guttering: eaves gutters are the most common; parapet gutters appear in older houses and are usually part of the roof structure; valley gutters run along the junction of two roof slopes. There are various shapes of eaves guttering to choose from. I personally think the ogee (a slightly squarer shape) is the prettiest, but the cheapest and easiest to clean is the half-round. Choose a style that suits the house. You may also want to consider adding lightning conductors or leaf guards.

FASCIA BOARD If the fascia (wooden plank on which the guttering is screwed) is rotten, you need to remove the guttering to replace it. It is safer and quicker to work off scaffolding. Before fixing the new board, clean out any debris built up behind it. You can repaint a fascia without removing the guttering but if you do remove it you will get a much better finish.

Blocked gutters can cause thousands of pounds worth of damage. Clearing them is one of the cheapest and easiest bits of home maintenance you can do.

SEE DAMP AND PESTS p152–157 ▶

ROOF EXTRAS	£	££	£££
GUTTERING PER METRE			
Cast iron	£13	£18	£22
Plastic ogee	£2	£3	£8
Plastic half-round	£1	£2	£4
Cast aluminium	£13	£15	£17
Rolled aluminium	£5	£10	£12
DRAINPIPES, PER METRE			
Cast iron	£13	£18	£22
Plastic	£2	£3	£7
FASCIA BOARD, PER METRE	£3	£5	£8

TRADES YOU WILL NEED

BUILDER/ ROOFER

3 DAYS, to replace the fascia and all the guttering around an average 3-bed house.

SEE BUILDERS p18–19, ROOFERS p22–23 ▶

⌂ REPOINTING

'Pointing' is the mortar used between bricks. If it has been applied badly or become worn by the weather, it can start to let damp into the house.

MORTAR If you can find someone who's happy to repoint with lime mortar, this is best because the lime enables the wall to move and breathe better and takes the force of any weathering. Cement is commonly used but it isn't porous and the bricks eventually wear away round it. I would always insist on using lime and sand mortar unless it is for a new build.

REPOINTING involves scraping out existing mortar with an electric chisel or a grinding wheel. Traditionally, bricklayers would use a hammer and chisel, but modern tools are less likely to damage the brick because you can get a much finer cut.

POINTING STYLES There are various pointing styles, such as tuck pointing, rubbed joints, bucket handle joints or hollow key, struck, weathered, and recessed key. It is important to match the rest of the building otherwise the result can look very peculiar.

ACCESS The more inaccessible the wall, the more you are likely to have to pay. Weigh up the relative costs before starting. If the repointing is on the first storey of your house, it can be done from a ladder but the builder will cover fewer square metres per day because they will be constantly climbing up and down the ladder. It is very much quicker to work from scaffolding.

FOR A FLAT WALL	£	££	£££
Pointing, per square metre	£20	£30	£40
Repointing, per square metre	£30	£40	£50

TRADES YOU WILL NEED

BRICKLAYER

A bricklayer can repoint 5–8 sq metres per day (including raking out) depending on the wall which means that it costs £15–20 per square metre.

SEE BRICKLAYERS p18–19 ▶

⊕ BRICKLAYING

Don't be bamboozled by the vast array of different bricks available. They can be broken down into a few basic types. Most are made of clay, kiln-fired and sold in pallets of 450 – although you might be able to buy smaller quantities. As well as walls, they can also be used on the ground to make paths, terraces or driveways.

BRICK TYPES Facing bricks are used for exposed brickwork. They can be 'wire cut' (cut with a wire like a bit of cheese) before they are fired, 'stock' (made in a mould, dried out and fired), 'handmade' (made in a mould but not compacted by a machine so they come with a distinctive creasing known as a 'smile'), or 'fletton' (made in distinctive clay from East Anglia). Of those types, handmade bricks are the most expensive. Commons are cheaper bricks and generally go unseen beneath render or plastering, in foundations or as the inner wall of a cavity wall. Engineering bricks are the toughest of all and have a high resistance to frost and water. Cheapest of all, and least attractive, are cement or calcium silicate bricks. Specials or specially shaped bricks are most often used for decorative work. Seconds or reclaimed bricks have been salvaged from old buildings and cleaned up.

COLOURS AND TEXTURES vary widely. Colour depends on the type of clay, whether any chemicals are used during manufacture, and the length of time for firing. Texture can be rough or smooth, either as a characteristic clay or because the bricks are marked by the manufacturer. Different coloured bricks can be used for decorative effects. Most bricks are solid, with flat sides or 'frogged' (with a dent to key the bricks). Sometimes they are cored or perforated (with holes through to act as a frog).

CHOOSING AND LAYING BRICKS Bricks are rated for durability in the face of frost, which can make them crumble. Frost-resistant bricks (F) are suitable for use in coastal regions, below ground or in cold areas. Moderately frost-resistant bricks (M) are mostly used between the damp-proof course and the eaves. Non-frost resistant bricks (O) are most suitable for internal walls. Soluble salts in bricks can eat away at mortar or cause white powder to appear on a wall. Soluble salt content is rated as low (L) or normal (N).

BRICKLAYING Each row of bricks is known as a course. They way they overlap is referred to as the bond. Bricks can be laid in three basic ways – stretcher (with the longest side or 'stretcher' showing), header (with the end or 'header' showing), on edge (the bricks are turned on their side). The most common way of laying bricks is the stretcher bond, which is made up entirely of stretchers and produces a wall half a brick thick. Combining the different methods can make decorative patterns. The most popular are: English bond, which alternates courses of stretchers and headers; Flemish bond, which alternates headers and stretchers within each course; English garden wall bond, where courses of headers are separated by three or four courses of stretchers; Flemish garden wall bond, where the headers in each course are separated by three stretchers; herringbone bond, where the stretchers are laid at alternating angles; and basket bond, where the stretchers are laid to look like basketweave.

An average of fourteen people are killed each year by falling off a ladder. The Health and Safety Executive has issued guidelines on how to use ladders safely (see www.hse.gov.uk). Do not expect your builder to take risks and be prepared for scaffolding if necessary.

MORTAR Traditionally, lime mortar was used to bind bricks. Today, a mortar of cement, lime and sand is most commonly used although sometimes the lime is swapped for a proprietary plasticizer. The mix must be in the right proportions so the mortar is close to the same strength as the bricks.

BUILDING COSTS	£	££	£££
Rebuilding a chimney	£1,300	£1,700	£2,500
Build a 9-inch 3x20ft retaining wall abutting the pavement	£600	£750	£900
BRICK COST PER 1,000			
Facing bricks	£300	£450	£600
Commons	£250	£325	£400
Engineering bricks	£300	£375	£450
1st class reclaimed bricks	£450	£525	£600

BEWARE: old imperial sizes (2⅝ or 3in) won't match the new metric size of 65mm.

TRADES YOU WILL NEED

BRICKLAYER

£250–500, per 1,000 bricks laid (120 bricks per square metre).

SEE BRICKLAYERS p18–19 ▶

🏠 FRONT DRIVES

Creating a front drive from scratch may mean that you need to get planning permission for the new access from the public road, from your local council. You will need permission if the access is on to a classified road, or likely to cause a traffic safety problem; if the property is a flat or maisonette; if the access is associated with works that needed planning permission; if you are widening an access; if you are making the access through an existing wall or hedge. If you are at all uncertain, it's wise to double-check with the local planning office.

CHOOSING A DRIVE The choice of covering for a drive will probably be dictated by the character of the house and its location, whether it is traditional or contemporary, in town or country. Some surfaces won't work on a hill (for instance loose gravel) or very uneven ground (for instance brick paving). It's worth comparing prices from several different specialist driveway suppliers, because this is an area where many people get thoroughly ripped off. Drives take a lot of wear and tear – far more than paths only used by pedestrians – and specialist companies should have the skills to ensure a new drive will last.

▶ **SHINGLE OR GRAVEL** comes in various colours and sizes (from 6mm to 20mm). It has great advantages for security, because it makes a noise as you walk across it. However, it's illegal to use shingle with new builds because wheelchairs have difficulty getting across it. If it's big enough shingle tends to stay where it is laid (use 18mm), whereas smaller grades tend to spray up when a car drives over them. Shingle or gravel are not good solutions for a sloping driveway unless you use concrete as a base, brush tar over it and roll the shingle on top, brushing off the excess. This will look like a shingle drive but won't slip to the bottom of the slope or spray over the grass. Another variation is self-binding gravel which is cheap, low maintenance and doesn't spray up easily. It's most suitable for a country house.

▶ **TARMACADAM** is an excellent, long-lasting, tidy solution. Red tarmac can look good too, and comes in a number of shades, but is a little more expensive than the usual black. Surfacing contractors usually charge by area, but on a small job such as a drive, will probably charge by the hour for a team of four men. Use a reputable contractor who will lay the drive properly, so that it will last well. A badly laid drive will soon crack and quickly show signs of wear and tear.

➥ **PATTERN-IMPRINTED CONCRETE (PIC)** has numerous finishes and colours and can look like stone, brick, tiles, cobbles or even decking, to name just a few of them. Bear in mind that it is a big job to lift concrete once it has been laid, so if anything goes wrong with drainage or gas pipes running underneath the drive, you can be in for problems.

PIC can look great, but will need maintenance. Weeds will grow in the joints if they are left untended and it should be regularly swept so lichen doesn't get a hold. This drive covering must be laid properly or it will sink or crack, or the surface may flake. I would always recommend that you hire a specialist company and check out their previous work. Costs can vary wildly so it is also sensible to get several quotes before deciding which company to use.

A **badly laid drive** will soon **crack** and quickly show signs of **wear and tear!**

▶ **BRICK PAVING** is a more expensive solution than many other types of driveway, because it is much more labour-intensive to lay. Because bricks are not always exactly the same dimensions, laying them is fiddly and therefore time-consuming and expensive. Laid in patterns, bricks can look lovely – for example, herringbone angled at either 90° or 45° stretcher bond, basket bond or interlocking patterns that use different colours. The colour of an individual brick can be a monotone or it can be multicoloured, giving a softer effect. The choice is bewildering, but let the character of the house and its environment guide you towards making the right one. Clay bricks are very hard-wearing – they can last for centuries and their colour will not fade. Brick paths are prone to moss and can get very slippery so need occasional cleaning with a high-pressure hose. In time, you may also need to do a bit of weeding to tidy up between the pavers.

▶ **BLOCKS** While bricks are mostly square or rectangular, blocks come in a wide variety of shapes. Bear in mind that blocks don't last as long as bricks, but they will still give you a good twenty years. There are also special-shaped pavers and endless variations in colour to choose from, although the colour will gradually dim in the sunshine. The different production processes for blocks and bricks make bricks the more expensive option. Blocks are usually exactly the same dimensions, so laying them is less time-consuming and labour-intensive than bricks.

➡ **CRUSHED LIMESTONE (SCALPINGS)** gives a rougher finish than the other options but is a good solution for a traditional country driveway. Roll the scalpings and cover with sand or gravel.

➡ **HOGGIN** is a mixture of clay, sand and shingle. Once it is put down and rolled, it provides an extremely hard finish. It also has the benefit of being very cheap.

Most drives that **crack up soon** after being laid have **inadequate foundations**. Ask your **local Building Regulations** Officer for **advice** on the foundations that are required.

FRONT DRIVES PER SQ M	£	££	£££
6mm pea shingle/gravel	£6	£7	£8
20mm shingle/gravel 50mm thick	£5	£6	£7
Self- binding gravel	£7	£8	£9
Tarmac 2-layer 20/50mm thick	£20	£30	£40
PIC	£18	£20	£23
Block paving	£30	£30	£40
Brick paving	£75	£100	£125
Crushed limestone	£30	£40	£50
Hoggin (100mm thick)	£8	£11	£14

TRADES YOU WILL NEED

SPECIALIST CONTRACTOR	**£60–£120 AN HOUR**, for a team of four men to prepare and lay a drive.
BUILDER	**£120–£180 PER DAY**, for a general builder to prepare and lay a drive.

SEE BUILDERS p12–15 ▶

⊕ NEW MANHOLES

There's rarely a need to change an old manhole, access or inspection chamber, but if you want to connect into an existing drain run or to have rodding access to any joints or bends, you will need a new one. The deeper and more complicated the connection, the more it will cost to put in.

CONSTRUCTION Generally, a domestic manhole needs to be no more than 600mm deep. If any brickwork is underground, engineering bricks should be used. Today, traditional clay pipes have given way to plastic piping and plastic chambers. Pipes should always be laid in straight trenches filled with pea gravel, with a manhole marking any change of direction. If plastic piping is being connected to clay piping, special joints are needed to accommodate the slightly different sizing of the pipes. The installation of any part of a drainage system must meet building regulations, so involve your Building Inspector.

MANHOLE COVERS are most often made of iron or galvanised steel and usually come with the manhole frame. If you are putting one in the middle of a driveway, patio terrace or indoor room, you can get a recessed tray cover and put the ground finish over it. Old manhole cover can also be replaced with these. Bedded in concrete, so that the top lip of the tray is flush with the ground, the tray can be filled with gravel, bricks, tarmac or even turf, so that it blends in completely with its surroundings. The most common size used in a domestic setting is 450x600x90mm (18x24x3.5in) although other sizes are available.

MANHOLES	£
MANHOLE COVER	
Plain	£50
Recessed tray	£75
Inspection/access chamber	£100

TRADES YOU WILL NEED

LABOURER

1–2 DAYS, to dig hole.

1 day for a bricklayer to build the inspection chamber.

SEE BUILDERS p12–15 ▶

⌂ NEW GARDEN FENCE

Fences provide a popular way of marking the boundary of a property. They are cheaper than a wall and quicker to erect. All fences need fixed posts at regular intervals to make them stable. The most commonly used are timber, concrete or metal. One way of fixing them is to use metal skewers (each topped by a square socket that holds the post), which are hammered into the ground. They're considered to be the easy way to do fencing, but I think they make it far more difficult to get an exact vertical line. I prefer posts to be bedded directly into the ground and stabilised with concrete. The taller the post, the deeper the concrete footing needs to be to hold it securely in place.

Don't have all the posts cemented in before attaching the panels, because you'll find the panels won't **fit the gaps** precisely.

PANELS Panelled timber fencing comes in all sorts of styles — such as closeboard, larch lap, picket, trellis and hurdles. There are other types of fence that don't come in panels, such as feathered edge, bamboo, or post and rail, which naturally will take longer to build because each piece of timber has to be dealt with separately.

INSTALLING A FENCE The key requirements of a fence are that it should be straight and vertical. The best way to achieve that is by using a piece of string to mark out where you want the fence to run. The easiest way to get a straight line is to put the posts and panels up alternately, propping up the posts with hardcore in the hole and wooden braces on the ground, using a spirit level to make sure they are straight. Then all the holes should be filled with concrete at the end of the job, sloping it slightly from the wood down to ground level so rain will run off easily. If you are using timber, treat it with a preservative.

To help **prevent rot**, run gravel boards along the base of the fence or **leave a gap** above the ground.

FENCING	£	££	£££
POSTS			
Metal posts	£18	£21	£32
Wooden end/corner/inter	£3	£7	£18
Concrete end/corner/inter	£10	£15	£23
PANEL 1.8X1.8M (6X6FT)			
Timber	£12	£25	£50
Willow	£15	£30	£50
Bamboo	£15	£25	£45

TRADES YOU WILL NEED

CARPENTER

This is a job much better done by two people. Expect them to put up about ten panels a day. If the fence is not already constructed in panels, expect them to do the equivalent of six panels a day.

SEE CARPENTERS p20–21 ▶

⬣ LAYING A PATIO

To get the best results, planning a patio or decking should be done as carefully as if you were adding another room to your home. Position, size and materials are critical.

POSITION What time of day will you be using it most? This will help you decide on the direction it should face to get the most sun or, if there's a choice, which side of the house it should be on. As a basic rule of thumb, choose east for breakfast and morning; south for all day use; and west for late afternoon or early evening. Strong prevailing winds may dictate a sheltered position. Do you want it to lead off a particular room? Are there any trees to take into account to provide shade or privacy, or that will have to be removed? Check the location of pipework or manholes, since access to them will have to be factored into your considerations. Also look at the fall of the land – it will be more expensive if a slope has to be built up. How large do you want the patio/deck to be? This will depend on what you are using it for and, to some extent, on the size of your garden. Try to keep things in proportion. If you plan to have eat outside, make sure it's large enough for people to sit comfortably round a table as well as being able to walk around it without stepping off the edge.

PATIO MATERIALS The next major consideration is which material to use. Stone slabs, concrete slabs, imitation stone, or bricks? If laying a new patio near the house, choose a colour that complements or contrasts with the brickwork. Dark colours will make the patio look smaller, but they will absorb the light so there will be less glare and any heat will be retained and radiated as the evening cools down. Combinations of different coloured stone can be used to good effect, or the same coloured stone can be laid to create patterns – as of course can bricks (See Bricklaying, page 171). The more complex the pattern and the more the slabs have to be cut, the more expensive the job will be.

PREPARATION Before laying stones or bricks, the ground will have to be properly prepared by levelling it and laying a sound, solid foundation, usually of hardcore or scalpings. These two areas of preparation are key to a successful patio. Without them, the patio might crack or sink in places. Make sure the patio lies below the level of the damp-proof course. There should be a very slight slope away from the house so that rainwater is drained off. A newly laid patio should not be used for about three days so that it has time to settle. In the meantime, cover it with polythene and occasionally sprinkle it with water so the pointing (if used) doesn't dry too fast.

DECKING The great advantage of a deck is that it can go where no patio can. It has a wooden sub-structure or frame so it can be raised anything from 150mm (6in) to high above the ground. Decks can be built over a slope, uneven ground or even water.

PREPARATION Raised decking means the frame will have to be fixed to vertical posts that are embedded in concrete footings to give the deck stability. If using softwood (the most popular option in the UK and cheaper than hardwood) make certain that it is tannalised (treated with preservative) and guaranteed to last for between ten and twenty-five years. Generally, standard-length decking boards range in width between 75-150mm (3-6in) and are grooved so that they don't become too slippery when wet. The grooves should run the same way as a slight slope built into the deck, so that any water runs off them easily. The boards can be laid in different ways to create patterns too (vertical, horizontal, diagonal, chevrons). It's important to decide on the pattern you want BEFORE the frame is made so that the joists of the frame are in the right place. To prevent weeds from growing underneath the deck, cover the ground below the frame with black plastic before it is installed.

COSTS PER SQ M	£	££	£££
PATIO			
Approx 4.2x4.2m (14x14ft)			
Ground levelled, paving patio laid and pointed	£50	£60	£70
SOFTWOOD DECK			
Approx 3x3m (10x10ft)			
Local joiner	£34	£50	£150
Local decking company	£90	£120	£150
National decking company	£83	£90	£120

TRADES YOU WILL NEED

BRICKLAYER

3–4 DAYS, to install a 4.2x4.2m (14x 14ft) paved patio.

CARPENTER

4 DAYS, to install a 3x3m (10x10ft) deck.

SEE BRICKLAYERS p18–19, CARPENTERS p20–21 ▶

INDEX

Thanks to:

Steve at A1 Lofts, Balham Glass, Clare Barber, Barry and Steve at Base Flooring, Richard and Diccon Beeny (as always), Fanny Blake, Marie Clayton, Katie Cowan, Abby Franklin, Laura Hill, Andrew Howard, Katie Hudson, Carly Madden, Colin and Steve Moulds, Polly Powell, Reed Harris Tiles, Paul Stevens, Gemma Wilson, and my dear long-suffering husband Graham.

Project Editor: Carly Madden
Design Manager: Gemma Wilson
Production Controller: Morna McPherson
Design: CB-Design
Editor: Marie Clayton
Indexer: Margaret Vaudrey